TABLE OF CONTENTS

USEFUL TOOLS IN THIS GUIDE

Look for these at the top of each zone page. They are designed to give you a quick reference to some of the key elements in your decision-making process.

ATES

ATES 1 ATES 2 ATES 3

The majority of backcountry tours in this book cover terrain that the Avalanche Terrain Exposure Scale (ATES) rates as 1–Simple. These routes, as defined by ATES, are: "Exposed to [or use] low angle or primarily forested terrain. Some forest openings may involve the runout zones of infrequent avalanches. Many options to reduce or eliminate exposure. No glacier travel." A small number of our selected routes use terrain with greater avalanche exposure than ATES 1, though we recommend only skiing these routes during times of exceptional stability. *To learn more about ATES, visit the Parks Canada website at* **pc.gc.ca/en**

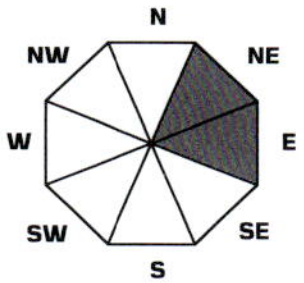

General Aspect
The general direction all runs in a particular zone will face.

° ‘ **Max Slope Angle / Descent Elevation Loss**

SYMBOLS

Avalanche Terrain Information

Parking, Trailhead, Skintrack Start

Access, Ascent, Skin Information

EXIT **Exit Information**

P **Parking Lot / Area**

Dog Information

Pass Information

I'd like to dedicate this book to my wife Lisa and son Louie.

Throughout what is now the bulk of my career as a ski mountaineer and writer, they've inspired me to ponder, write about (and, I hope, demonstrate) a safer mindset. They're as much the source of the "safe tours" concept as I.

Thank you.

Any guidebook, or for that matter a book of any sort, is in the end a group effort. A big thanks to Alex Neuschaefer for the cover photo and numerous aerial images, and to the local experts we sent to odd corners of the earth to get just the right terrain photo: Gary Smith, Trevor Bona, and Dennis Sovick. Thank you to Keitha Kostyk for the graphic design, Farid Tabian for the cartography, and Emma Walker for editing. Albert Fiorello offered much regarding the Front Range routes, Aaron Mattix contributed the Rifle beta, and Rohan Roy corroborated numerous route descriptions across the state. Publisher Andy Sovick ground-truthed numerous routes. Finally, we couldn't have produced this book without the help of the Beacon Guidebooks authors who believe in this project, and understand the need to synchronize information between the various Beacon guidebooks and maps. They contributed text for certain route descriptions (credited herein), and were always available to help with fact-checking: Rob Writz, Josh Kling, and Stephen Bass.

About the Author **Lou Dawson**

Lou Dawson is a widely published author and professional blogger who writes about backcountry ski touring and mountaineering. He wrote his first of many books over thirty years ago. Lou was the first person to ski all 54 of Colorado's 14,000-foot "fourteener" peaks in 1991—a feat that was not repeated, despite numerous attempts, for sixteen years. With more than a half-century of ski touring behind him, Lou continues to explore the winter backcountry for the joy of athletic movement, spiritual awe, and fellowship with family and friends. **Learn more at LouDawson.com**

Cover Alex Neuschaefer Greg, Matt and Sarah Steinwand

Published by Beacon Guidebooks, Gunnison, Colorado **Printed in Canada.**

FOLLOW
THE VOICE
DIRACT VOICE: WORLD'S FIRST BEACON WITH VOICE NAVIGATION.
CLEAR COMMANDS, INTUITIVE DESIGN, EASY HANDLING.
Find out more on ortovox.com
"RUN STRAIGHT!"
45
DIRACT VOICE
ORTOVOX

BACKCOUNTRY RULES + ETHICS

This atlas should in no way substitute for good judgement or sufficient experience. While there are no universal laws of backcountry ethics, there are widely accepted practices for traveling in the winter backcountry.

While backcountry skiing, I will:

- ✔ leave no trace.
- ✔ check the avalanche forecast for the local area.
- ✔ park at the trailhead with space-saving in mind.
- ✔ try to follow the most established skintrack to my destination, thereby leaving the slope as un-tracked as possible.
- ✔ find a different skintrack or route if I feel the established route is unsafe.
- ✔ communicate well and respectfully with other parties.
- ✔ respect designated areas, trail use signs, and established ski tracks.
- ✔ not block the trail when stopping.
- ✔ not disturb wildlife and will avoid areas posted for their protection or feeding.
- ✔ not litter. I will pack out everything I packed in.
- ✔ realize that my destination and travel speed are determined by my equipment, ability, terrain, weather, and traffic on the trail, and will plan accordingly.
- ✔ promote a friendly and positive attitude while in the backcountry.
- ✔ respect traffic and avoid putting uptracks in runs.

Backcountry Gear Checklist:

- ✔ skis / splitboard
- ✔ boots / poles / skins / ski crampons / ski & skin wax
- ✔ goggles / insulating hat / gloves (light)
- ✔ helmet
- ✔ transceiver / probe / shovel
- ✔ map / compass / GPS-cell phone / radios
- ✔ shell / puffy jacket / warm gloves / buff
- ✔ food, water, sun protection, lip balm
- ✔ sunglasses
- ✔ headlamp / extra batteries
- ✔ first-aid kit
- ✔ repair kit / tarp-rescue sled
- ✔ consider parking permits & passes
- ✔ post-activity snacks, water and beverages
- ✔ trip itinerary left with friend and under car seat
- ✔ sun-shielding hat for bright days

AVALANCHE SAFETY IS CRUCIAL FOR ANYONE RECREATING IN THE MOUNTAINS.

Nearly every winter, avalanches kill more people in Colorado than any other state in the United States and have a significant impact on the state's highways. We selected the tours in this book for their minimal avalanche danger, but each tour should still be treated as avalanche terrain. This means you must always carry the standard equipment and have a modicum of training in its use, as well as in how to recognize and avoid avalanche terrain. Our overarching criteria for safer routes is that they offer reduced slope angles, usually around 30° or less. While conventional wisdom is accurate in considering such angles to be significantly safer from avalanches, there are documented instances of fatal avalanches occurring on such slopes, as well as slides falling from steeper terrain above. This book is not intended as an avalanche safety treatise, but we can share a few overarching principles: educate yourself; don't blunder; be willing to change your plans; if in doubt, hire a guide.

GET THE FORECAST

CAIC

CBAC

KNOW THE ROAD CONDITIONS

CDOT

NORTH AMERICAN AVALANCHE DANGER SCALE

EXTREME
Avoid all avalanche terrain.

HIGH
Very dangerous avalanche conditions. Travel in avalanche terrain not recommended.

CONSIDERABLE
Dangerous avalanche conditions. Careful snowpack evaluation, cautious route-finding and conservative decision making are essential.

MODERATE
Heightened avalanche conditions on specific terrain features. Evaluate snow and terrain carefully; identify features of concern.

LOW
Generally safe avalanche conditions. Watch for unstable snow on isolated terrain features.

NO RATING
Watch for signs of unstable snow such as recent avalanches, cracking in the snow and audible collapsing. Avoid traveling on or under similar slopes.

Winter travel in mountainous terrain, including skiing, snowboarding, snowmobiling and climbing, is dangerous in nature and can result in serious injury or death. Read and understand this warning before using this publication. Beacon Guidebooks has made an effort to confirm that the information shown on this publication is correct. High Point Productions, DBA Beacon Guidebooks is in no way responsible for damage to property, personal injury, trespassing or violation of law in conjunction with the use of this publication. User accepts and takes responsibility for all risks. Discrepancies between trail and route location and actual may exist. This publication does not depict private property. Routes drawn do not imply that public access is available. Information is subject to change faster than this publication can update. Liability is expressly disclaimed.

ALL BEACON GUIDEBOOKS PRODUCTS USE THE ATES SYSTEM

ATES (Avalanche Terrain Exposure Scale) is a planning tool designed and used extensively in Canada. It helps identify appropriate terrain for the avalanche hazard of the day, but it does not predict the stability of a given slope. *Source: Parks Canada*

Our authors characterize and classify the terrain of each sector of their backcountry zone. Once classified, we fit them into one of five categories: **0-Non-avalanche**, 1-Simple, 2-Challenging, **3-Complex**, 4-Extreme. The definitions are below. These **white**, **green**, **blue**, **black**, and **red** colors **should not be confused** with the difficulty of a run (like we are used to seeing in a ski resort). **Green** means: Simple avalanche terrain. **Blue** means: Challenging avalanche terrain. **Black** means: Complex avalanche terrain. **Red** means: extreme avalanche terrain.

ATES 0

0 - Non Avalanche

No known exposure to avalanches. Very low-angle or densely forested slopes located well away from avalanche paths, or designated trails/routes with no exposure to avalanches.

You will almost never see this rating in our books, since nearly everything backcountry ski related will be near avalanche terrain.

ATES 1

1 - Simple Zones

Exposure to low-angle or primarily forested terrain. Some forest openings may involve the runout zones of infrequent avalanches and terrain traps may exist. Many options to reduce or eliminate exposure.

Simple Routes offer options to reduce your exposure to avalanche terrain in **Challenging Zones**.

ATES 2

2 - Challenging Zones

Exposure to well-defined avalanche paths, starting zones, terrain traps or overhead hazard. With careful route finding, some options will exist to reduce or eliminate exposure.

Challenging Routes offer options to reduce your exposure to avalanche terrain in **Complex Zones**.

ATES 3

3 - Complex Zones

Exposure to multiple overlapping avalanche paths or large expanses of steep, open terrain. Frequent exposure to overhead hazard. Many avalanche starting zones and terrain traps with minimal options to reduce exposure.

Complex Routes increase your exposure to higher consequence terrain. Sometimes Beacon rates an individual route in challenging terrain as a complex route.

ATES 4

4 - Extreme Zones

Exposure to very steep faces with cliffs, spines, couloirs, crevasses or sustained overhead hazard. No options to reduce exposure; even small avalanches can be fatal.

Extreme Routes increase your exposure to higher consequence terrain. Sometimes Beacon rates an individual route as an extreme route.

Head to the education page on our website to learn more about ATES, and to practice using it.

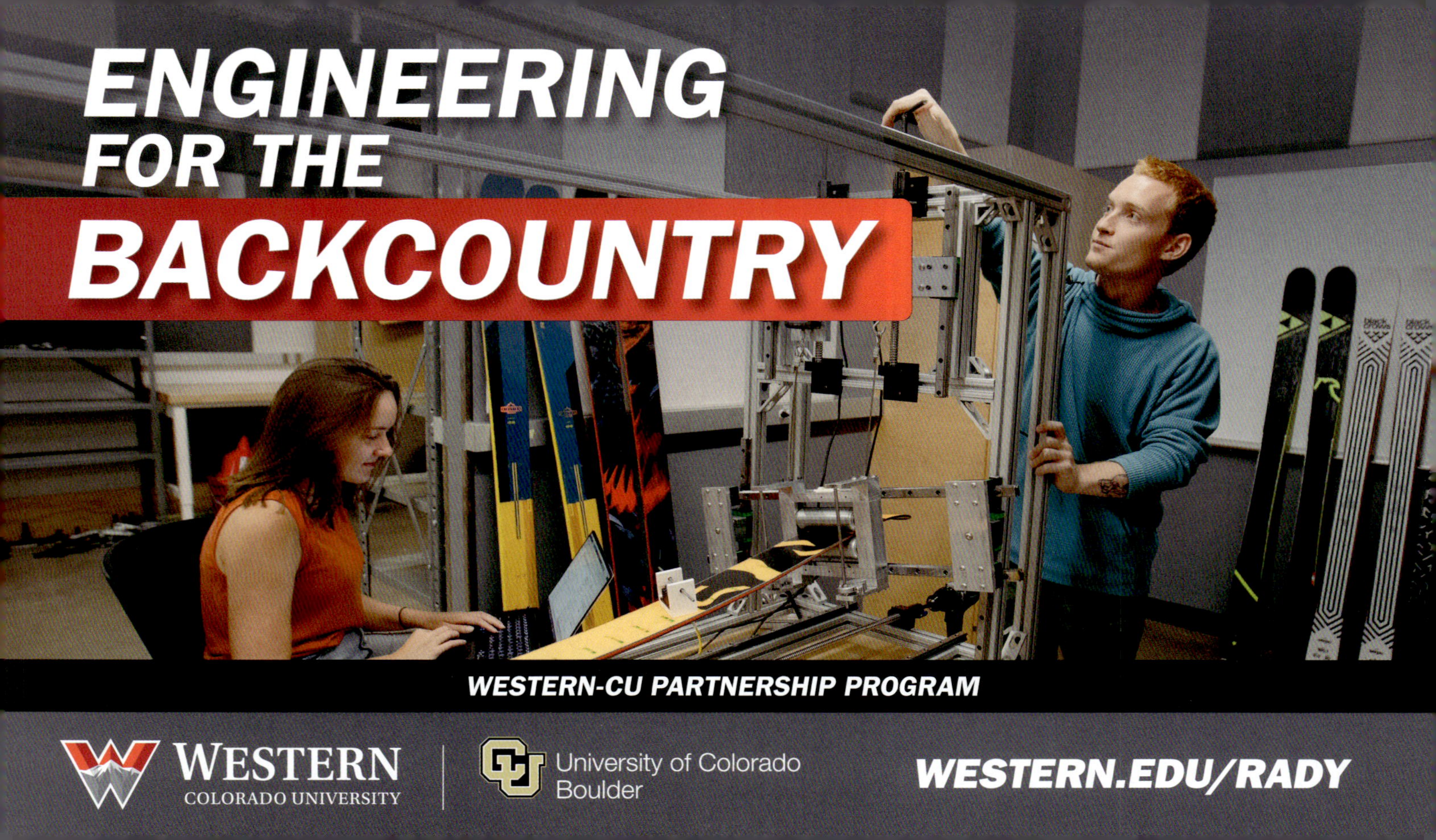
ENGINEERING
FOR THE
BACKCOUNTRY
WESTERN-CU PARTNERSHIP PROGRAM
WESTERN
COLORADO UNIVERSITY
University of Colorado
Boulder
WESTERN.EDU/RADY

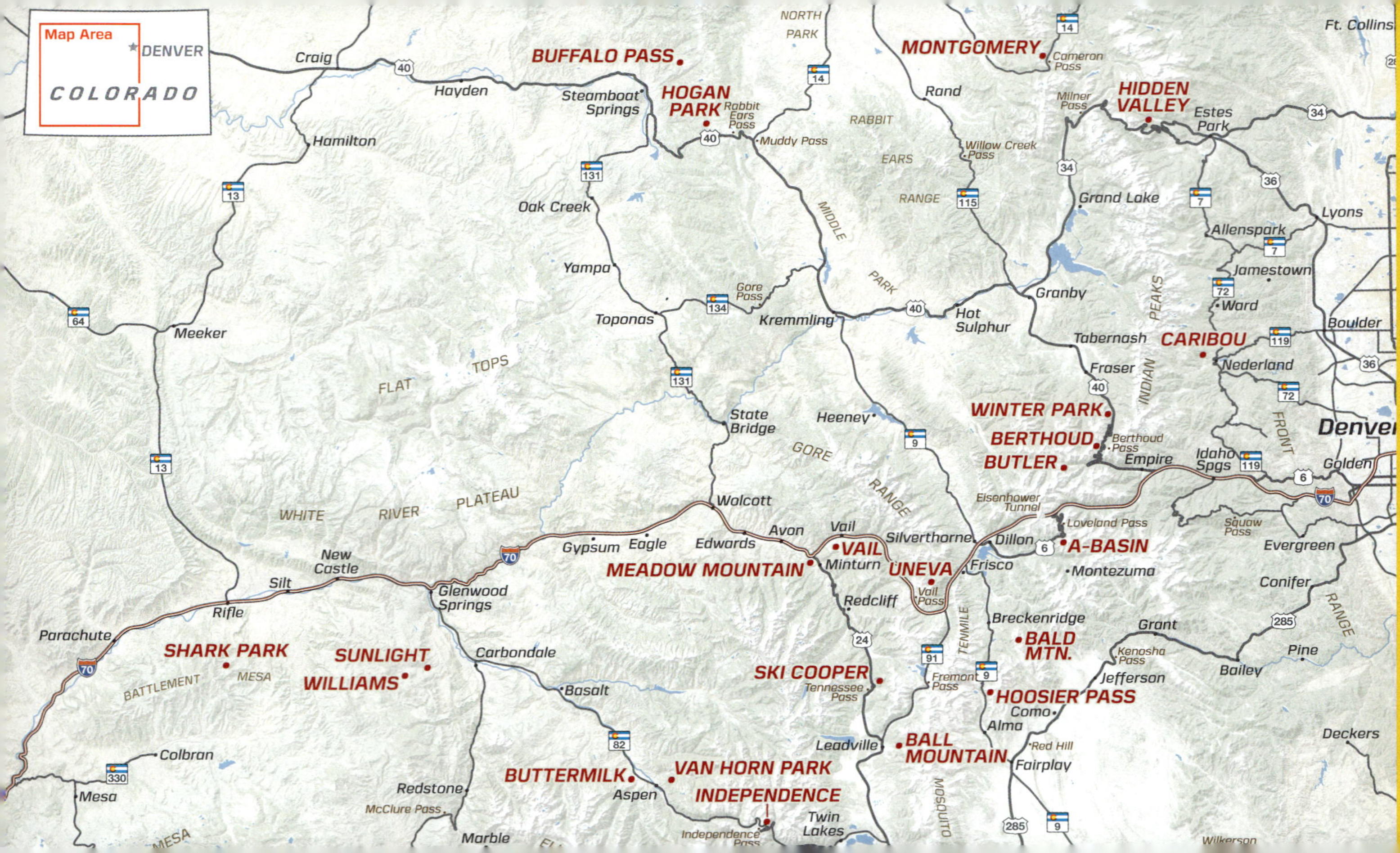
Map Area
DENVER
COLORADO
BUFFALO PASS
HOGAN PARK
MONTGOMERY
HIDDEN VALLEY
CARIBOU
WINTER PARK
BERTHOUD
BUTLER
A-BASIN
VAIL
UNEVA
MEADOW MOUNTAIN
SHARK PARK
SUNLIGHT
WILLIAMS
SKI COOPER
BALD MTN.
HOOSIER PASS
BALL MOUNTAIN
BUTTERMILK
VAN HORN PARK
INDEPENDENCE
Craig
Hayden
Steamboat Springs
Rabbit Ears Pass
Muddy Pass
Hamilton
Oak Creek
Yampa
Toponas
Gore Pass
Kremmling
Hot Sulphur
Granby
Rand
Willow Creek Pass
Cameron Pass
Milner Pass
Estes Park
Grand Lake
Allenspark
Lyons
Jamestown
Ward
Boulder
Tabernash
Nederland
Fraser
Denver
Golden
Idaho Spgs
Empire
Berthoud Pass
State Bridge
Heeney
Meeker
Wolcott
Avon
Vail
Edwards
Eagle
Gypsum
Silverthorne
Dillon
Frisco
Minturn
Vail Pass
Eisenhower Tunnel
Loveland Pass
Squaw Pass
Evergreen
Montezuma
Conifer
New Castle
Silt
Rifle
Glenwood Springs
Parachute
Carbondale
Basalt
Redcliff
Breckenridge
Grant
Pine
Bailey
Kenosha Pass
Jefferson
Fremont Pass
Tennessee Pass
Como
Alma
Red Hill
Fairplay
Leadville
Deckers
Colbran
Mesa
Redstone
McClure Pass
Aspen
Twin Lakes
Independence Pass
Marble
Wilkerson
Ft. Collins
NORTH PARK
RABBIT EARS RANGE
MIDDLE PARK
INDIAN PEAKS
FRONT RANGE
GORE RANGE
TENMILE
MOSQUITO
FLAT TOPS
WHITE RIVER PLATEAU
BATTLEMENT MESA
MESA
40
14
131
134
115
34
36
7
72
119
6
70
9
24
91
285
82
330
13
64

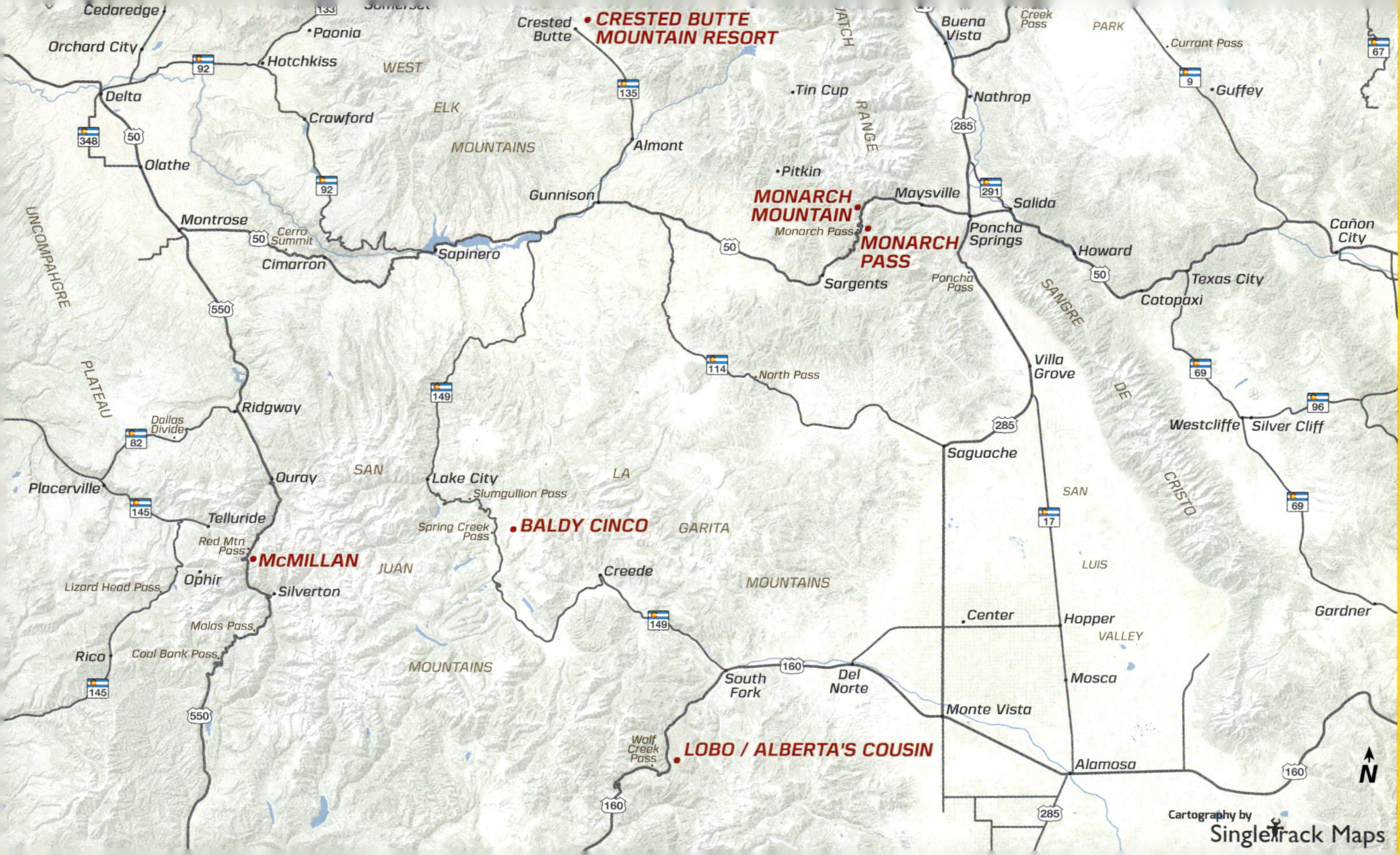
CRESTED BUTTE MOUNTAIN RESORT
MONARCH MOUNTAIN
MONARCH PASS
BALDY CINCO
McMILLAN
LOBO / ALBERTA'S COUSIN
Cedaredge
Paonia
Orchard City
Hotchkiss
Delta
Crawford
Olathe
Montrose
Cerro Summit
Cimarron
Sapinero
Gunnison
Crested Butte
Almont
Tin Cup
Pitkin
Buena Vista
Nathrop
Maysville
Salida
Poncha Springs
Monarch Pass
Sargents
Poncha Pass
Howard
Texas City
Cotopaxi
Cañon City
Currant Pass
Guffey
Creek Pass
PARK
WEST ELK MOUNTAINS
SAWATCH RANGE
UNCOMPAHGRE PLATEAU
SANGRE DE CRISTO
SAN JUAN MOUNTAINS
LA GARITA MOUNTAINS
SAN LUIS VALLEY
Ridgway
Dallas Divide
Ouray
Placerville
Telluride
Red Mtn Pass
Ophir
Lizard Head Pass
Silverton
Molas Pass
Coal Bank Pass
Rico
Lake City
Slumgullion Pass
Spring Creek Pass
Creede
North Pass
Villa Grove
Saguache
Westcliffe
Silver Cliff
Center
Hopper
Mosca
Gardner
South Fork
Del Norte
Monte Vista
Wolf Creek Pass
Alamosa
92
50
348
135
285
291
550
149
114
82
145
17
69
96
160
9
67
N
Cartography by Singletrack Maps

Dry Lake Campground
1
2
3

ATES 1

BUFFALO PASS QUAKER BOWL

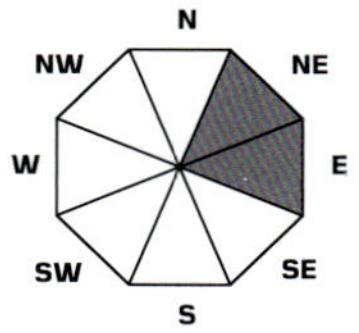

Also known as “Aspen Bowl,” this beginner zone boasts beautiful, naturally gladed aspen trees. Users can enjoy relaxed-angle glades extending from the Quaker Bowl overlook down to the Spring Creek drainage. All of the runs in this area take the fall line. Quaker Bowl is an attractive tour due to its proximity to Dry Lake Campground. Nonetheless, this is the lowest-elevation ski zone on Buff Pass. With a thin, early-season snowpack, the willows at the bottom of the run can be fierce. (Much of the text in this route description was sourced and revised from Beacon Guidebooks’ *Backcountry Sled-Skiing: Buffalo Pass, Colorado*, with the permission of author Stephen Bass. We thank him for helping keep our information consistent and accurate.)

Exploring too far skier’s right can result in skiing far below the common return track, and can take you far down into the Spring Creek drainage and consequent avalanche terrain. Keep the bottom snow road in sight and don’t descend below it.

All Buffalo Pass tours begin at Dry Lake Campground—a busy winter trailhead, primarily used by snowmobilers and the local cat-skiing operation. You’ll feel out of place without a snowmobile, but the Quaker Bowl terrain is within easy reach of the light tour skier. Driving from Steamboat Springs: Navigate to Fish Creek Falls Road, then head north on Amethyst Drive. Stay on Amethyst until it becomes Routt County Road 36, and look for signs indicating Buffalo Pass. Turn right onto State Road 38, and drive about ten minutes to Dry Lake Campground.

From Dry Lake, skin the main snow road for 1.5 miles to Lila’s corner, which is a sharp turn through a gully. Just past Lila’s corner, there is a steeper shortcut snow road to your left. Do not take the shortcut road. Instead, continue to the right on the main road, and Quaker Bowl Road is your next possible right turn. Skin Quaker Bowl road to the next right turn. From there you’ll begin climbing along the top of Quaker Bowl with the runs below you. An alternative approach option is to skin the snow road for 0.5 miles, then turn right (southeasterly) and climb the north side of the hill.

EXIT

Climb northeast out of Spring Creek to the low saddle you crossed on your approach. Enjoy another lap or return to the trailhead.

1 WAGON LANE — 29° — 745’

Wagon Lane provides options to skier’s far right. Do not ski farther right than the route shown in our photo. If you do, you’ll end up in steeper terrain with more avalanche danger.

2 CREAKY SPRINGS — 29° — 486’

Creaky Springs is a fall-line ski without much to think about other than vegetation. During times of thin snowpack, beware of the horribly thick willows at the bottom of the run, to skier’s right. Plan your line accordingly.

3 SHORTY — 25° — 355’

Shorty is an enjoyable beginner skier’s tree run. The aspens are more open than those of other lines. Keep the road to your left as a navigational boundary.

Mt. Werner
You are entering the Steamboat Ski Area
and are subject to the Colorado Skier
Safety Act. Hogan Park skiers are
welcome to ride Morningside Lift one time.
If you choose to continue on the
Hogan Park Trail, follow the blue
diamonds to the ridge. Be cautious of
downhill skier & snowboarder traffic.

HOGAN PARK TRAVERSE

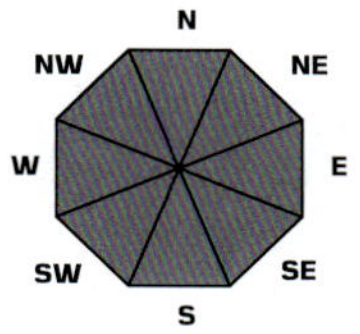

Hogan Park is a scenic, lengthy, one-way cross-country adventure ending at Steamboat Ski Resort. There are few chances for backcountry turns along the way, but this beautiful backcountry tour rewards you with a long in-bounds descent.

Time:	3–6 hours
One-Way Tour Distance:	7 miles from Rabbit Ears Pass to the Ski Resort boundary and Morningside Lift. 11.5 miles to the Steamboat base area.
Elevation Gain:	1,553'
Elevation Loss:	4,094'
Elevation Gain and Loss:	+4,400' - -4,400'

Equipment Note: As this tour includes a descent of Steamboat Resort, consider "randonee" or "skimo" gear that's on the light side of the weight spectrum. Such gear is overkill for the lengthy low-angle portion of the route, but rewards you with an enjoyable descent of the resort. Nordic ski touring equipment is adequate if you're comfortable using it to descend resort slopes. Steamboat Ski Resort requires ski leashes or brakes.

The suggested route completely avoids avalanche terrain. It is possible to accidentally deviate from the route and encounter small, steep slopes that could pose a hazard. The more prevalent danger with this route is that of becoming lost. This would be hard to do on a peaceful sunny day. But in the event of a blizzard, the undulating terrain of Hogan Park can confuse even the savviest navigator. Carry a map, compass, and GPS, along with the knowledge to use them. Consider using our Rakkup app on your phone for offline GPS navigation.

Park or get dropped off at the large parking lot on the south side of the highway, 2.5 miles west of the sign indicating Rabbit Ears Pass. You'll see a brown Forest Service sign on the north side of the highway that states "Hogan Park Trail." You are skiing one-way to Steamboat, so arrange a shuttle.

First Section of Route: Begin with a gentle climb to the north past the trailhead sign. You'll immediately notice the diamond-shaped blue trail markers nailed to trees. While these markers can be found the entire length of the tour, don't rely on them entirely; some may be missing. Ski northerly for about 2 miles, then travel just east of north for the second section of the route. The first half of the tour loses more elevation than it gains.

Middle Section of Route: On a clear day, once you're about a third of the way through the tour, you'll catch glimpses of Mount Werner. At 3.2 miles, you'll reach and cross a gully. After a short ski through a forest, climb gentle slopes to a flat valley speckled with beautiful (or windy) meadows.

Last Section of Route: While meadow-hopping the final stretch to Mount Werner, keep a keen eye out for the blue markers, and check your GPS. At the ski area boundary, you'll see a sign stating: "You are entering the Steamboat Ski Area and are subject to the Colorado Skier Safety Act. Hogan Park skiers are welcome to ride the Morningside Lift one time. If you choose to continue on the Hogan Park Trail, follow the blue diamonds to the ridge. Be cautious of downhill skier and snowboarder traffic." Help us all maintain Steamboat Ski Resort's good vibes and generosity by obeying their rules and offering a smile!

Descending the Resort: Skiing from the top of Morningside Lift to the base area is somewhat intuitive, but you can end up on several lengthy catwalks. For better skiing, follow these runs to the base area: Over Easy, Calf Roper, Rainbow, Ego, then BC Skiway catwalk. When you reach the base, pause for a frothy beverage at Slopeside Grill.

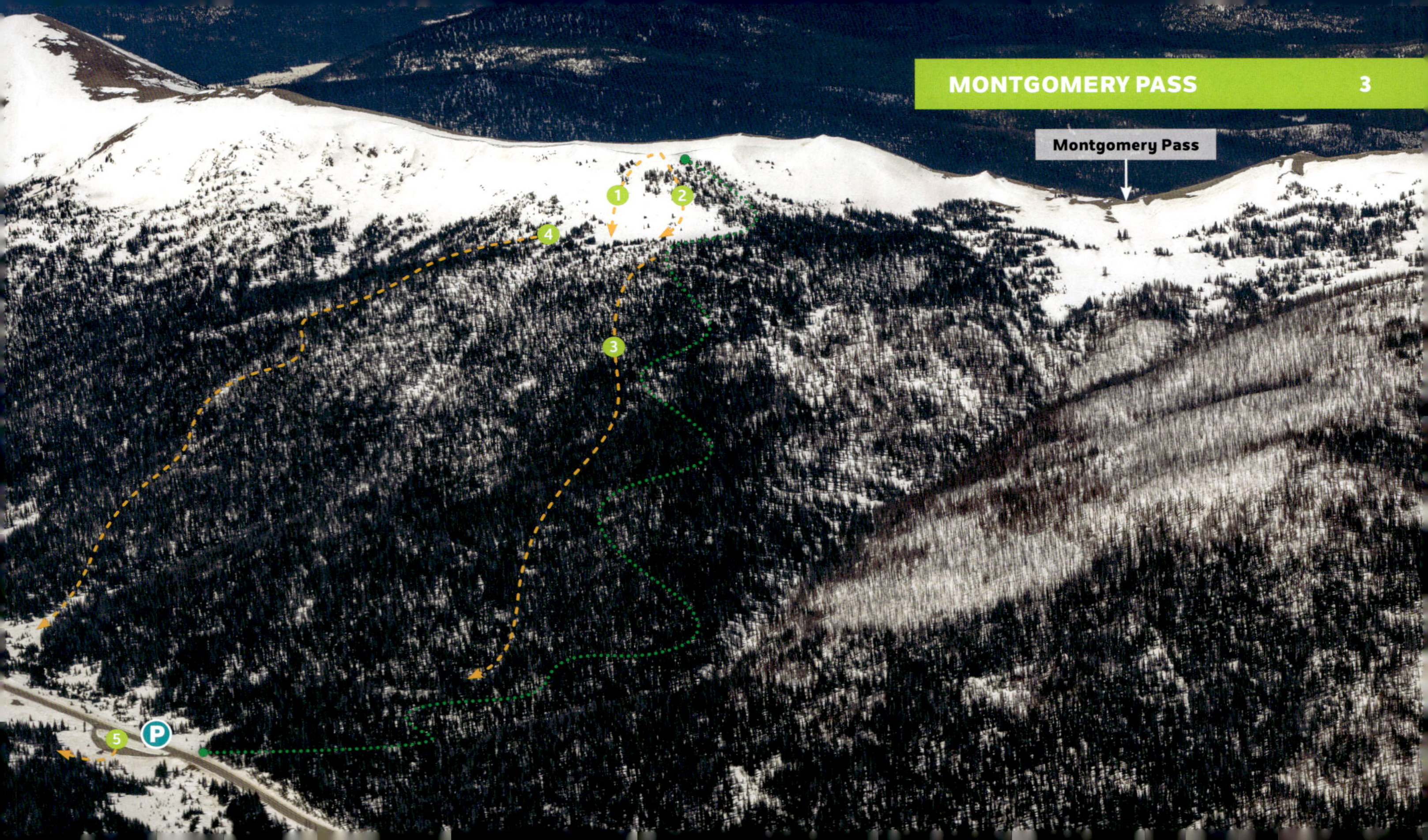
Montgomery Pass
1
2
3
4
5
P

ATES 1

MONTGOMERY PASS

Cameron Pass provides access to a large area of backcountry in northern Colorado, accessed from Hwy. 14. Montgomery Pass Trail requires advanced ski skills due to a steep, narrow return through the forest after you enjoy open bowls above. Some of the information here was sourced and revised from Beacon Guidebooks' *Backcountry Skiing Cameron Pass, Colorado*, with the permission of author Rodney Ley. We thank him for helping keep our information consistent and accurate.

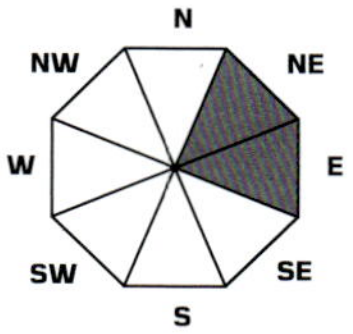

To avoid alpine terrain and steeper bowls, stay below timberline by turning around at 11,000'. For skiing on the steeper, open slopes above, you'll need experience in evaluating avalanche terrain and conditions.

Park at the Zimmerman Lake Trailhead, 1.4 miles east of Cameron Pass. As of this writing, parking is free and bathroom facilities are available.

From the parking lot, walk across the road and find Montgomery Pass Trail, marked with blue diamonds and a sign. Ski up the Montgomery Pass trail 1.5 miles to timberline. To avoid nearly all avalanche danger, stop at 11,000' and ski back down the trail (which is somewhat steep and narrow, and can thus be difficult for novices). Beware of uphill traffic. To continue to the top, climb through a patch of stunted trees and find the lowest-angle slope leading to the summit of the unnamed knob at 11,400', just south of Montgomery Pass.

EXIT

Descend near the skintrack. To prevent colliding with folks headed uphill, try to avoid descending in the skintrack. No matter your choice of our suggested routes, you'll land near Hwy. 14, within 0.25 miles of the parking lot.

1 MONTGOMERY BOWL RIGHT — 31° 380'

To ski the bowl, reach the knob at 11,400' and descend due east towards the prominent bench, skier's left of a steep gully. This is avalanche terrain.

2 MONTGOMERY BOWL LEFT — 31° 380'

While not particularly steep, this is avalanche terrain, so study conditions and terrain before you commit. Descend from the knob, slightly left, aiming for the place where your approach route meets the trees.

3 MONTGOMERY FOREST — 27° 1,020'

This route generally follows the skintrack back down. Try to avoid descending directly in the skintrack to avoid collisions with folks heading uphill. Get creative and enjoy the tight trees, seeking fresh cold snow. A helmet can help battle the branches in the forest.

4 EXPLORER'S GLADES — 27° 1,000'

This route is more exploratory in nature, and the thick trees can be annoying. But it is a nice way to leave the beaten path and seek out the occasional open glade. Descend skier's right of the tight, timber-choked gully. The route finishes in the flat meadows upstream of the parking lot. Re-apply your skins for the 0.25-mile slog back to parking.

5 ZIMMERMAN LAKE TRAIL

For the ultimate in low-angled, avalanche-safe tours, the Zimmerman Lake Trail (not pictured) explores terrain from the parking area. Follow obvious signs. Note that this trail has little to no terrain for downhill turns. Nordic ski gear is appropriate.

Round-trip: 3.5 mi

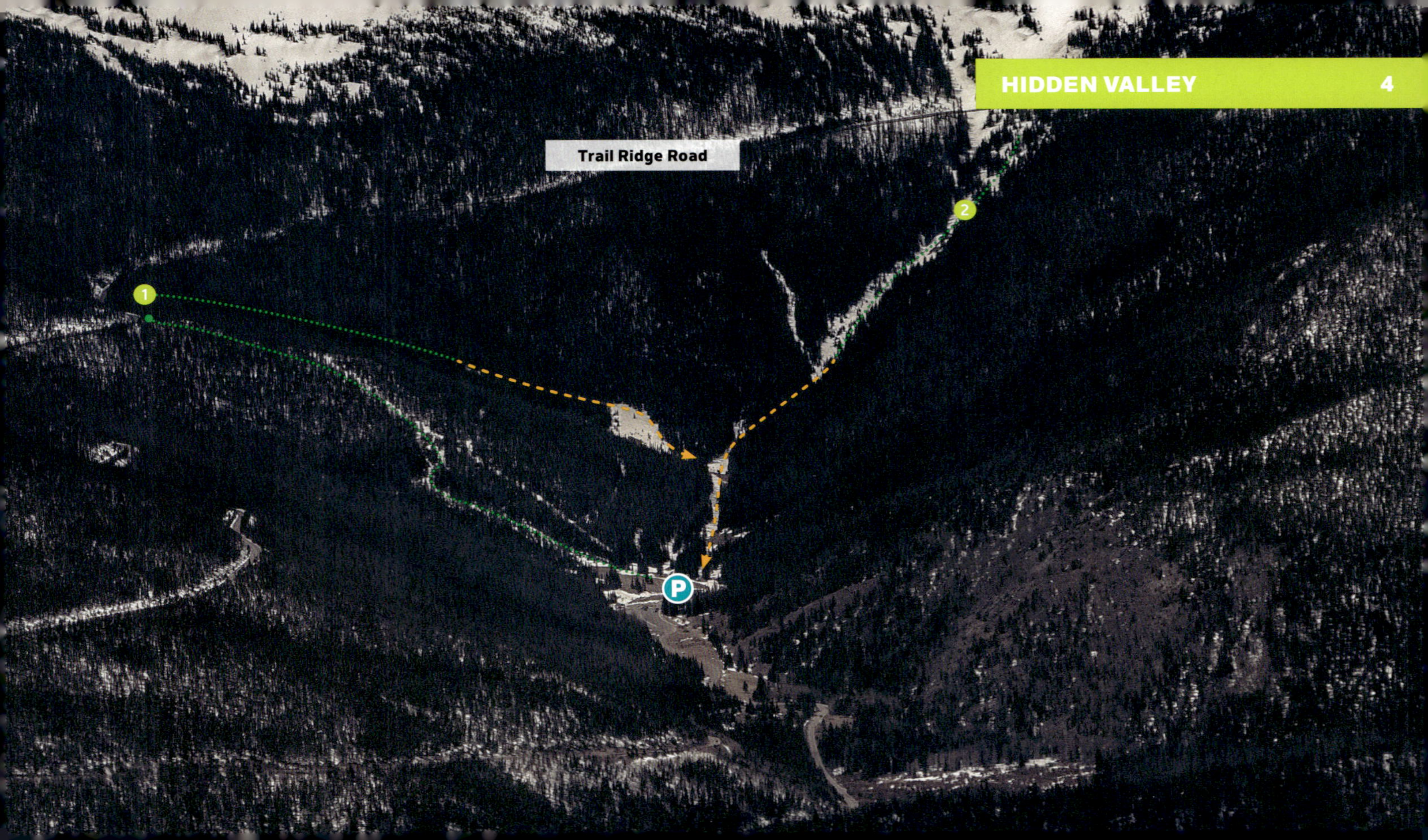
HIDDEN VALLEY
4
Trail Ridge Road
1
2
P

ATES 1

HIDDEN VALLEY

Colorado is replete with a number of decommissioned "ghost" ski resorts. Given legal public access, the cut runs of such resorts often provide a variety of low-angled tour options, and road access may be excellent. The Hidden Valley ski lifts spun from 1955 to 1991 and were subsequently removed. Enjoy what has become a free, human-powered ski area! Some of the information here was sourced and revised from Beacon Guidebooks' *Backcountry Skiing Rocky Mountain National Park, Colorado*, with the permission of author Mike Soucy. We thank him for helping keep our information consistent and accurate.

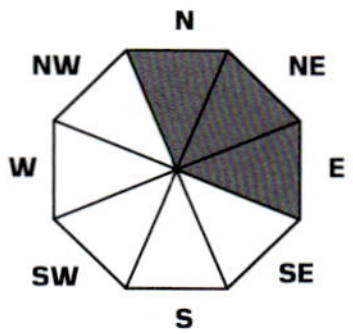

These tours use the ski runs formerly comprising the Hidden Valley ski resort in Rocky Mountain National Park. To minimize avalanche danger, stick with the lower-angled runs in the timber below Trail Ridge Road. You may see numerous ski and snowboard tracks in the terrain above Trail Ridge Road. While these upper slopes are commonly viewed as avalanche-benign, understand that this is avalanche terrain.

From the east (Denver, Boulder), follow US Hwy. 36 or Hwy. 34 to Estes Park. Continue on Hwy. 36 west out of Estes Park and enter Rocky Mountain National Park (fee) at the Beaver Meadows Entrance. Continue on Hwy. 36 for 3 miles to a fork. Take a left onto Trail Ridge Road. When you hit another fork in 2.5 miles, turn right onto the Hidden Valley Road. (There was no sign here as of spring 2021, but it's the only turn at this mileage.) Follow the Hidden Valley Road for about 0.25 miles to the parking lot at the Visitor Center and sledding hill. Note that Trail Ridge Road is closed for winter a short distance above the Hidden Valley turnoff. The road opens later in the spring, and is a popular way to access corn snow skiing.

Apply climbing skins at the Visitor Center and ski the well-beaten, obvious path leading up the Hidden Valley Creek drainage. If you aim to ski down Aspen, climb up the Aspen run, staying to the side in order to preserve the powder for downhill skiers. For the lightest tour, don't climb up Aspen—simply stay in the Hidden Valley Creek drainage all the way to Trail Ridge Road, then turn around and descend the Valley Run.

EXIT

Return to the parking area via the approach trail.

1 ASPEN — 22° — 710'

Just 0.4 miles from the Visitor Center, your first option is Aspen: a wide, low-angled run to skier's left (in a conifer forest). You can climb Aspen 0.5 miles to Trail Ridge Road, but the upper half of the route passes through tight timber that can make for difficult downhill skiing. For the easiest skiing, turn around where the timber closes off the ascent. To make a loop of it, continue up to Trail Ridge Road and ski westerly on the snow-covered road 0.8 miles to intersect and ski down the Hidden Valley Creek drainage (Valley Run) to the Visitor Center.

2 COLUMBINE — 25° — 1,060'

From the Visitor Center, skin a mile westerly up the Hidden Valley Creek drainage, to Trail Ridge Road, then descend your ascent route.

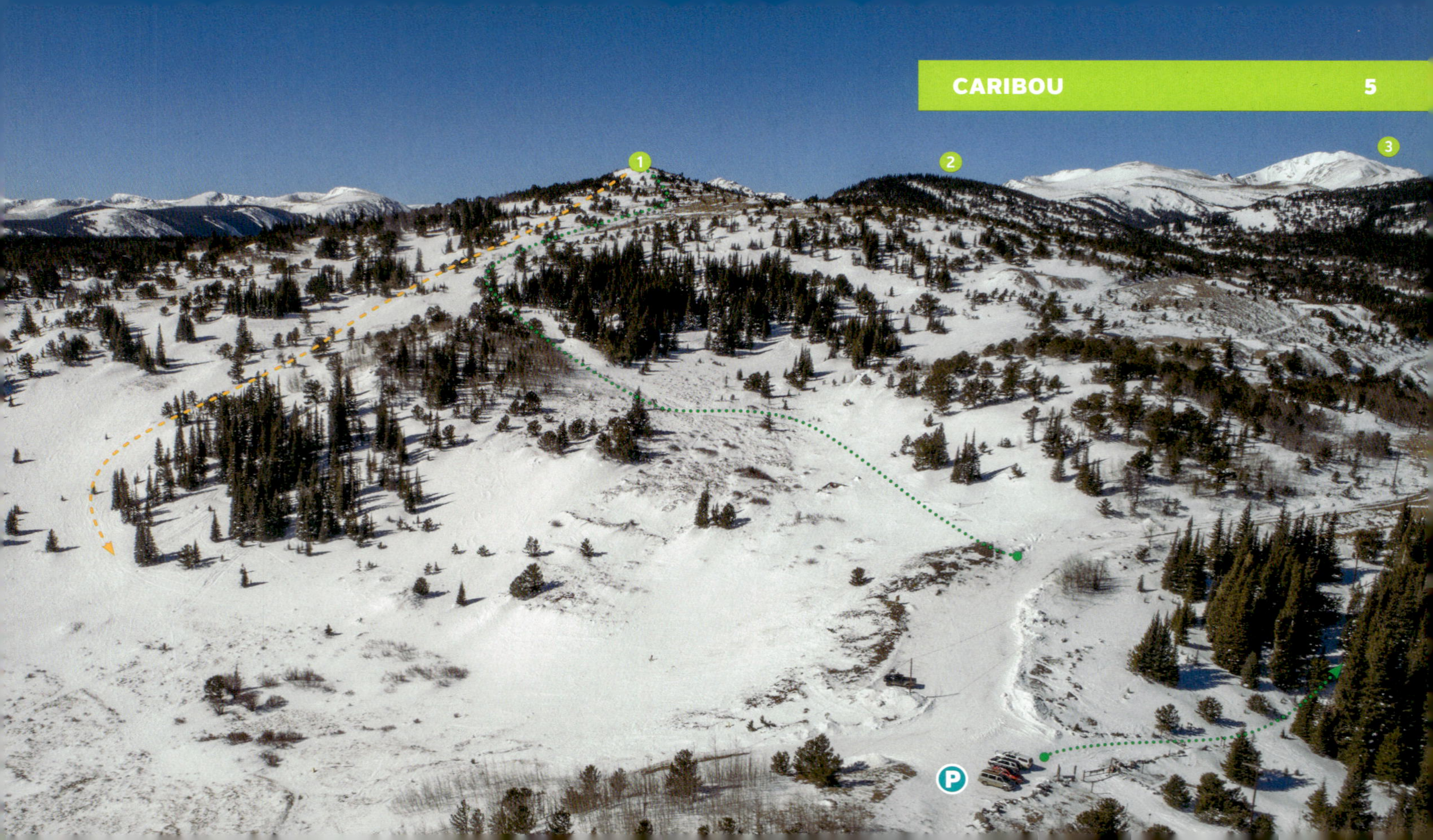
CARIBOU
5
1
2
3
P

ATES 1

CARIBOU

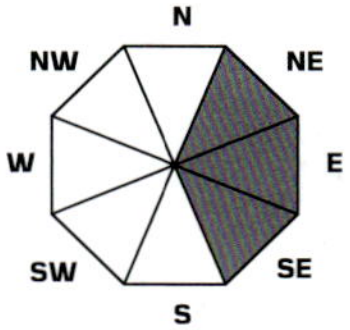

The Caribou area provides closer options for skiers hailing from the populous Front Range cities. Consequently, parking can be a problem. Arrive early and carpool if possible. As with most other regions on this side of the Continental Divide, high winds can cancel your plans. A tour in the forest and then lunch in Nederland can save your day.

Avalanche terrain does exist in this area. Stay off steeper slopes and do not venture into Klondike or Caribou Glades (Bald Mountain) during Considerable or High hazard ratings. A few cornices form on Klondike ridge, and avalanches are possible on the area's steeper, open alpine terrain. Stay on lower-angled slopes for less danger.

From Boulder, drive west up Hwy. 119 (Boulder Canyon) to the small town of Nederland. GPS your way through Nederland to Caribou Road. In detail: Boulder Canyon Road leads to the only roundabout in Nederland. Take the west road out of the roundabout, AKA West 2nd Street, AKA State Hwy. 72. Note the fire station on your left. Just past the fire station, turn left on what Google Maps shows as Road 128. Follow 128 (Caribou Road) 5.3 miles to the snow closure, which will hopefully be at the higher parking area (10,000'), but winter maintenance may vary. Good tires and 4x4 are recommended.

EXIT

Return to the parking lot via your approach route. You may want to re-apply skins for the last (slightly uphill) section of Road 505. Consider linking up the other descents on your way back.

1 CARIBOU HILL — 27° — 500'

This obvious climb next to the parking area needs little description. Please use existing skintracks to avoid depleting the powder. If you're breaking trail (rare), stay to the side of the good downhill lines. At the bottom of your descent, traverse back to the parking lot, or descend a little farther and hike back up.

KLONDIKE APPROACH *(image next page)*

From the parking area, start without skins on the snow-covered, slightly downhill Road 505, then apply skins when the route begins to climb. To identify Road 505, look for a gate and sign on the north side of the parking area. Pass mine buildings and stay left on Road 505. About a mile from the parking area, swing southerly to the top of Klondike Peak.

2 KLONDIKE DESCENT *(image next page)* — 27° — 565'

Descend northeast. During your return, look for turns to be made by skiing glades on the northeasterly reaches of Klondike. Or simply follow high ground northwest off Klondike, and eventually ski down to the approach road.

CARIBOU GLADES APPROACH *(Bald Mountain)* — 30° — 1,460'

Again, ski Road 505, but take a right at an obvious fork 0.25 miles from the parking area. Continue 0.75 miles on a mine access road to just below timberline on Bald Mountain. The skintrack then continues climbing about 800 vertical feet next to the ski slopes on the east shoulder of Bald Mountain. Most people strip skins at about 11,000', where the snow cover gives way to wind-scoured rocky terrain.

3 CARIBOU GLADES *(Bald Mountain)* — 27° — 800'

Descend east through thin glades. Rack up a few laps.

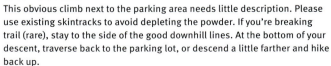

CARIBOU (KLONDIKE)
5.1
1
2
3

Bald Mountain
3
To Trailhead

1
2
3
4
5
P

ATES 1

BERTHOUD PASS EAST SIDE

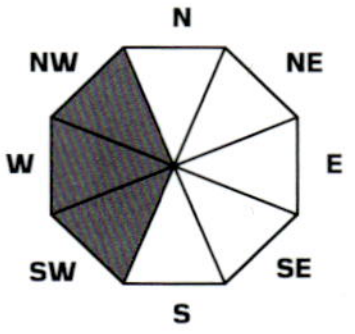

In the Colorado Front Range region, Berthoud Pass is arguably the best place to find accessible ski touring. At the Continental Divide west of Denver, Berthoud often catches more snow than other Front Range touring areas. And the variety of exposures helps you find slopes protected from snow-damaging wind. However, make no mistake: this is a windy place, as is most of the Front Range. The lines directly above the parking lot on Mines Peak are mellow and a good place to take someone who is new to backcountry skiing. By mid-winter, kickers built on these slopes provide entertainment. (Much of the text in this route description was sourced and revised from Beacon Guidebooks' *Backcountry Skiing: Berthoud Pass, Colorado*, with the permission of author Rob Writz. We thank Rob for helping keep our information consistent and accurate.)

The East Side provides a variety of low-angle terrain. Venturing beyond the summit of Mines Peak, or skier's right into Hell's Half Acre (left side of picture) will bring you into complex avalanche terrain.

East Side skintracks begin at the Berthoud Pass parking lot.

Gain the runs above the parking lot, Bonanza, Bell Trail, and CDT East, by following the CDT East Trail up a gentle, snow-covered road. Climb Colorado Mines Peak by ascending climber's left of the runs. There's often a skintrack above Powder Line that ascends the gentle slopes to the road switchback below the summit.

EXIT

East Side routes end at the parking where you began.

1 COLORADO MINES PEAK — 20° — 622'

Mines Peak remains windswept for most of the season. Yet the big upslope storms of spring may drop enough sticky snow to make long descents possible from the summit. To avoid avalanche terrain, descend directly towards the parking lot.

2 POWDER LINE — 20° — 333'

Powder Line is on the looker's left side of the main run above the Berthoud Pass parking lot. The left side of this run holds the community skintrack. Be sure to turn around at the top of Powder Line, as the skintrack continues into avalanche terrain.

3 BONANZA — 20° — 366'

Bonanza is to the looker's right side of the main run above the Berthoud Pass parking lot. The tree-lined slopes in the upper portion are slightly steeper than the open area.

4 BELL TRAIL/DUNN'S RUN — 20° — 213'

This is the short, gladed tree run divided by the CDT East road and Bonanza.

5 CDT EAST — 20° — 131'

Yet another resort remnant, CDT East is the snow-covered road that's most often used as a skintrack to access this area. Pockets of low-angle tree skiing may be found between the first two road switchbacks.

Round-trip: 2 mi

110s
Teacup Bowl
1
P

ATES 1

BERTHOUD PASS THE 110s

This area, on the west side of Hwy. 40, comprises a great deal of avalanche terrain. The Perfect Trees route provides the least exposed skiing.

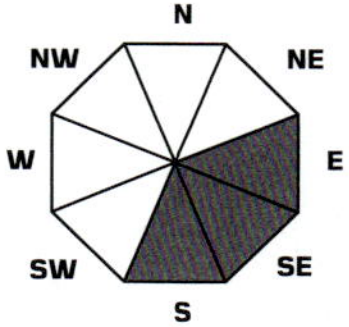

Quite a few tragic Berthoud-area avalanche accidents have occurred over the years. While you may see skiers on the steeper slopes, don't let that lull you into false security—every year, some of them end up as statistics. Be aware that you are in "real" backcountry. To avoid avalanche terrain, ski and climb on lower-angled terrain, use your ascent route as the general line for your return (assuming it's safe), and avoid passing too closely under Teacup Bowl, a steeper area to the south of Perfect Trees.

Current Creek Trailhead is the large turnout off of Hwy. 40 / Berthoud Pass Road, approximately 2 miles from the summit and 9 miles from Winter Park. There is a parking lot on the west side of the highway next to the start of the skintrack. Additionally, you'll find more parking just north and across Hwy. 40. This second lot may not be plowed after major storms.

The skintrack heads west into the trees from the southwest corner of the Current Creek parking lot. There is a road to the left—this is the exit from the 90s; don't let it mislead you. The skintrack soon splits with a west (left) line following Current Creek, going to the Hidden Knoll area. The right line (our recommended route) climbs steeply northwest through a clearing and then levels out; there is often another split here. The right track, recommended, usually climbs to the north around Tea Cup Bowl and switchbacks through Perfect Trees to 11,721'. This is your turnaround spot. Continuing the climb brings you to the challenging avalanche terrain of the Upper 110s.

EXIT

Descend to the Current Creek Parking lot by trending skier's right, through the trees at 11,100'. This is important, so use your GPS if in doubt, as trending any direction other than skier's right will put you into the 110s Cliffs.

1 PERFECT TREES

30° 921'

Descend the lower-angled areas of Perfect Trees southeast from the top. When you reach the bench at approximately 11,600', trend right beneath Teacup Bowl, then descend the general route of your skintrack back to parking. Much of this skiing is easterly-facing and may develop sun-crust soon after storms. Consequently, if you're looking for powder, ski during the colder months of winter. Otherwise, time your tours for corn snow. April and May, after a few days of sunshine, are your best bet for corn harvest. What about March? That's the iffy month for conditions. You might find powder during, or soon after, a March storm, but breakable crust can persist for many days.

1
2
3
P

ATES 1

BUTLER GULCH

Butler Gulch feeds a large area of alpine terrain with a few lower-angled tree skiing options. The access trail follows a summer jeep road; it's a nice walk and a breezy glide upon your return. To avoid avalanche terrain, reverse your tour in the gladed area at the end of the valley.

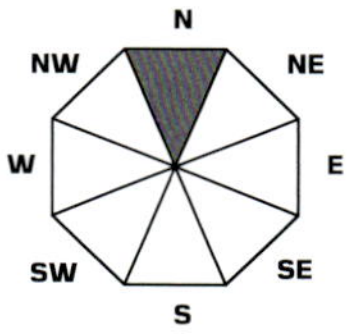

Avoid entering the runout zones and terrain traps of overhead avalanche terrain by staying below timberline. Be aware of your surroundings.

You'll be in avalanche terrain as soon as you break timberline or access steeper slopes. To keep it mellow, enjoy glades below timberline, accessed via the standard and well-used skintrack.

Thanks to the operations of Henderson Mine, the road to the snow closure and parking is consistently maintained. Drive I-70, take Exit 232, and drive Hwy. 40 a short distance through the town of Empire (slow down or receive a friendly piece of paper). Continue 7 miles and turn left on the well-signed Henderson Mine Road. Roll another 2 miles to the obvious trailhead parking. Note that motorized recreationists use the Jones Pass area northwest from the trailhead, while non-motorized users access the Butler Gulch area by heading south from the trailhead on a summer jeep trail. 4x4 is recommended for this trailhead.

From the parking lot, ski the Butler Gulch / Jones Pass road for a few hundred yards to a major Y-intersection. The sign here indicates Jones Pass to the right and Butler Gulch (your goal) to the left. After climbing the low-angled, snow-covered road through a forest for about 1.5 miles, climb south into an obvious gladed area. To avoid avalanche terrain, reverse while you're still below timberline.

EXIT

Return via your approach route.

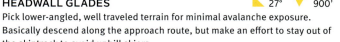

1 HEADWALL GLADES

27° 900’

Pick lower-angled, well traveled terrain for minimal avalanche exposure. Basically descend along the approach route, but make an effort to stay out of the skintrack to avoid uphill skiers.

2 CREEK CHUTE

27° 450’

Also known as Halfpipe Gully, this low-angle chute is lined with rock walls. Drop in from around 11,400’. As the trees tighten, traverse skier's right, back to the approach route.

3 BUTLER GULCH BOWL

30° 450’

While this is a wide, low-angle bowl, the large headwall above is a major avalanche slope. This poses an overhead hazard during unstable avalanche conditions.

Uneva Peak
East Uneva Peak
1
Corral Creek
To Vail
P

ATES 1

VAIL PASS UNEVA RIDGE

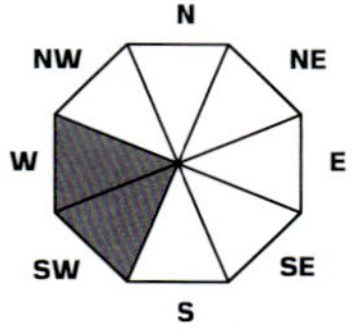

The Vail Pass backcountry, west of I-70, is virtually given over to motorized recreation in the form of snowmobiles, snowcats, and snowbikes. For peace and quiet, head for the easterly, non-motorized side of the highway. Here, you'll find terrain couched in the bowls and ridges of Uneva Peak. There's something for everyone, from springtime corn snow bowls to extreme north faces. For a moderate and fairly safe tour, the option described here works well.

Stay on lower-angled terrain. Avoid the temptation of existing skintracks that push your route higher and steeper, or expose you to steeper slopes that threaten from above. Pushing the route into avalanche terrain is appropriate if you have the skills and conditions dictate, but use your head.

Turn off I-70 at the Vail Pass exit. Be sure to buy a parking permit at the kiosk near the parking area entrance.

From the Vail Pass parking areas, walk the overpass east over I-70. Cross the pavement at the east end of the overpass and locate trailhead signs for the Corral Creek ski trails. Ski the Corral Creek Trail around the north side of Corral Hill. After a quick and somewhat level half-mile, you'll break out of the trees and have an easterly view of your destination: a low-angled glade area to the east-southeast. Prior ski tracks will likely indicate the route, but a GPS will provide assurance. Ski down a short hill to Corral Creek (leave your skins on), then climb easterly about 600 vertical feet and another half-mile to the top of obvious low-angled glades. Stop climbing at around 11,200' elevation, before exposure to steeper overhead slopes begins. The terrain beyond this point is threatened by avalanches from above.
Note: You can't see your final skiing destination from Vail Pass parking; it is hidden behind Corral Hill.

EXIT

Follow your approach route. Be aware that you're on high ground and could be tempted to descend farther below Vail Pass than you intend.

1 SOUTH UNEVA, LOWER SLOPES

29° 700'

Pick lower-angled, well traveled terrain for minimal avalanche exposure. Descend near the approach route, but make an effort to stay out of the skintrack to avoid uphill skiers.

1
2
3
P
I-70
To Minturn

ATES 1

MEADOW MOUNTAIN MINTURN

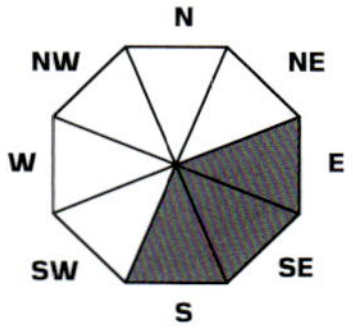

Meadow Mountain is a traditional destination enjoyed by everyone from dog walkers to snowmobilers, with a few sledders and skiers thrown in for good measure. You'll find quite a bit of lower-angled terrain here, though due to the exposure and vegetation, you'll need reasonable snow cover for acceptable skiing. Thus, your best months for this tour are probably January through March. Of historical interest, one of Colorado's earlier ski resorts existed here and ceased operation in 1970 as Vail began its rise to dominance.

A special note: Prolific backcountry skier Gary Smith, who snapped our photo of Meadow Mountain, died in an avalanche in 2021 in the backcountry adjacent to Beaver Creek Resort. We thank him for the enthusiasm he brought to our sport, and offer condolences to his friends and family.

Stay on lower-angled terrain. Note the few steeper slopes on the southeast side of Meadow Mountain to your right as you ascend the general route of the Line Shack Meadow Mountain Road.

Take Exit 171 off I-70 and drive south on Hwy. 24 for 0.25 miles. Use the turnoff just past the exit ramp, where you'll see parking for a sledding and tubing area, as well as a Forest Service facility. Meadow Mountain is a "shared use" area where you may encounter all types of winter recreationists. If using a route traveled by snowmobiles, stay to the side of the trail.

Avoid the sledding and tubing area (visible directly above parking) by skiing south on USFS Road 748 next to Hwy. 24 for about 0.25 miles. Continue following the general route of Road 748 as it swings around various switchbacks and terrain features on a gradual climb up Meadow Mountain, which is the ridge to your right as you're climbing. Stay on obvious, lower-angled terrain as you climb via the general route of the road. For a longer route, your turnaround or staging point is a building known as the "Line Shack" that's about 4.5 miles from the trailhead—but you can reverse anywhere. For ski terrain that's somewhat better quality than the meadows near the road, observe and conquer open areas on Meadow Mountain you'll see to your right (northwest) as you climb.

EXIT Follow your approach route.

1 LINE SHACK — 27° — 2,050'

If you're strong for the lengthy 4.5-mile approach, do your laps for turns on low-angled terrain in the vicinity of the Line Shack. Tip: While doing so is not within the purview of this book, it's possible to find human-powered skiing on the northwest side of Meadow Mountain, in the vicinity of the sledding/tubing hill and USFS facility. By all means, enjoy that option if it appears attractive and appropriate.

2 YOUR BACKTRAIL — 27° — 1,000'

For the most benign and least confusing route, descend near your ascent route.

3 ALTERNATE ASPECTS — 27° — 600'

A different aspect may hold different snow conditions; explore skier's left.

1
P

ATES 1

SHARK PARK RIFLE

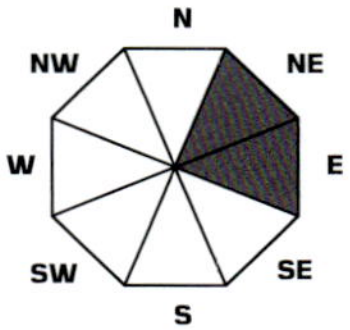

The Shark Park tour explores classic medium-altitude Western Slope aspen forests and meadows near the town of Rifle. The first part of the route follows the popular Beaver Creek summer trail, then deviates west and climbs the west side of the drainage to a high point in an open area known as Shark Park. Use of GPS is mandatory for newcomers. This is a mid-season tour, in shape from February into April, depending on the winter's snowfall. Check the Ski Sunlight snow report for a take on regional conditions. If Sunlight has 48 inches or more of base depth, Shark will be in good condition. Don't bother if Sunlight is below 38 inches.

Most of this area is too low-angled and timbered for avalanches to be a problem. Yet steeper and possibly dangerous pitches exist. Beware the small, tempting bowl dropping east from the summit. To avoid it, ski lower-angled terrain to the south along the ascent route.

Enter your destination as "Co Rd 317, Colorado 81650" in Google Maps. Leave I-70 at either of the Rifle exits (87 or 90), then follow Hwy. 13 south to a double roundabout. Zero out your trip odometer. At the second roundabout, take the first right turn onto South 7th Street/ Garden Lane. Drive 7th for 800 feet and continue through a sharp left turn. The street name is now Garden Lane / County Road 320. At 0.4 miles from the roundabout, turn right at a T-intersection and continue on CR 320, which is the Rifle-Rulison Road. At 2.8 miles from the roundabout you'll reach a Y-intersection. Turn left at the Y and drive Beaver Creek Road. You'll reach the first trailhead 8.1 miles from the roundabout (take a spur off Beaver Creek Road which leads a few hundred feet to a closed gate), or continue to the second trailhead 0.2 miles farther. Skiers often use the second trailhead, as the first may require walking a plowed, unskiable road. Safety note: These roads may have heavy energy-industry truck traffic. A section of the Beaver Creek Road narrows to one lane and oncoming trucks are always a possibility—proceed with caution. Parking is free, but limited. Regularity of maintenance and plowing may vary. As always, obey all signs.

From the second trailhead, ski a reclaimed former road 0.75 miles south up the Beaver Creek drainage. Continue up the drainage another 0.25 miles, then turn right and climb out of the drainage on a trail cut that switchbacks through an aspen forest. Leave the defined trail at about 8,700'. The remainder of the uphill route is less obvious. Look for a previous skintrack and use a GPS.

EXIT

Return via the approach route.

1 SHARK PARK DESCENT

30° 2,330'

End at the obvious high point of the Shark Park meadows. Enjoy good views from the summit conifer grove. Beware the cliff dropping abruptly to the north. If you find good skiing in the open areas, consider banging off a few short laps before braving the denser trees below. Note that local skiers work hard to keep the "skinner" separated from the downhill ski lines. Please follow suit, and use the existing skintrack if it makes sense to do so. Determine your best skiing options during the ascent. Most of the better descent terrain is in the general area of the uptrack. You're looking for an open aspen forest. A small amount of exploratory traversing might score you a few untracked turns, but take care to not stray into dense timber, or traverse so far your return to the valley is blocked by dense brush and trees.

Williams Peak
To Sunlight Peak
1
2
P

ATES 1

WILLIAMS PEAK GLENWOOD SPRINGS

Williams Peak is a small hill in the timbered terrain west of Sunlight Mountain Ski Resort. It's a good place to learn backcountry skiing, as well as a nice jaunt for experienced skiers who want a casual workout. The northerly slopes of Williams hold the most reliable snow, though much of the terrain is too forested for good turning. (Hint: during heavy snow years, a huge amount of excellent glade skiing may open up.) Williams is within the permitted ski area expansion area but thus far has remained backcountry.

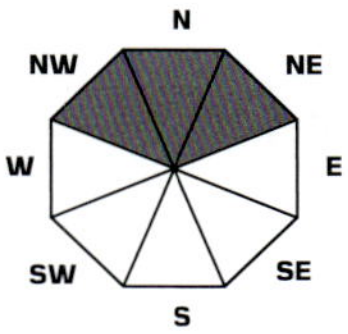

The obvious skiing on Williams is almost entirely in non-avalanche terrain. During less stable conditions, beware of small rollovers and cornices. This is heavily timbered terrain. Ski with a partner and stay in touch, as other hazards (such as tree wells) may exist.

Fourmile Road leads to Sunlight Mountain Ski Resort and Fourmile Park. Start from Grand Avenue on the south (Aspen) side of Glenwood Springs. Turn off Grand Ave. onto 27th street. Drive 27th through a roundabout, then a short distance to another roundabout. Take the south turn out of the roundabout onto Midland Avenue, then follow signs for Sunlight. At 10 miles from Glenwood, take a hard right turn on Road 300 (if you miss this turn, you'll end up at Sunlight). Drive 2.9 miles to roadside parking for Williams. To reach Fourmile Park, continue 1.7 miles up the road, which is usually closed by snow but may be plowed (8,880'). Please note: While ski touring on Williams Peak is a good bet, Fourmile Park is more of a motorized snowmobile venue than a ski touring area, so focus on Williams. While this is a popular snowmobile trailhead, snowmobiles are not recommended for assistance with this tour and are not allowed on Sunlight permit lands, some of which includes the Williams ski terrain.

From parking, walk a short distance up Fourmile Road and look for the skintrack heading left off the road. Skin south through timber. You'll soon enter a series of open areas leading to the summit ridge about 0.2 miles from the summit. Continue up the ridge to the apex.

EXIT

All the north side runs end on Fourmile Road. If your route choice doesn't lead directly to your parking spot, it's a simple matter to walk or skate the road.

1 ASPEN FORESTS 30° 1,320'

From the summit, trend northerly through meadows for a few hundred yards, then drop into a tightly gladed aspen forest. Consult your GPS to be sure you return to parking rather than ending up in the vast, forested area you'll encounter if you drop too far. We recommend exploring this route after you've skied Williams Glades and become familiar with the general Williams area layout. Note there may be a skintrack ascending this area.

2 WILLIAMS GLADES 30° 1,320'

From the summit, follow your approach route for a few hundred feet, then dive into a series of glades that lead down to the Fourmile Road. Finding your personal pow stashes might require a few laps.

3 SOUTH ASPENS BONUS *(not pictured)* 30° ~1,000'

From the summit, drop into open terrain and aspen glades towards Sunlight. Skin back to the summit and return to parking via the routes above. This run can be excellent during or just after midwinter storms; otherwise, it is quickly sun-damaged. During early spring, it's a good bet for corn snow.

To West Buttermilk
Lifts & Runs
Snowmass Resort
1
2

ATES 1

SUGAR BOWLS BUTTERMILK

Have some sugar with your milk. This classic ski tour is one of the best moderates around. You ski for a mile along a scenic ridge, then enjoy low-angled terrain that's safe from avalanches. **Note:** The return requires climbing 400 vertical feet from the bottom of your run, as well as reversing a mile of backcountry ridge. All additional fun.

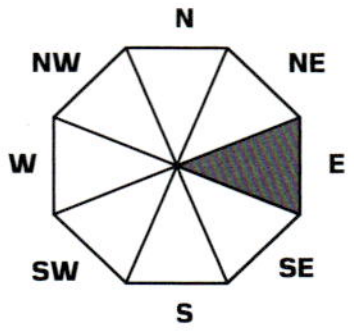

The recommended route is free of avalanche danger, but as always, pay attention to areas where you could stray onto steeper terrain below the access trail and to the west near Snowmass Resort.

Ride the lifts or uphill to the summit of Buttermilk Ski Resort.

From the resort summit, skin west along a mile of low-angled trail on a ridge. Enjoy this scenic walk, with various colored rocks of the maroon geologic formation forming a foreground to views of the high Elk Mountains. The Sugar Bowls are an obvious area of tilted meadows you'll reach after your forest walk. The first meadow you intersect, Sugar Spoon, isn't the main portion of the skiing, but it does connect. Strip skins here, or continue a few hundred feet to the top of the main bowls, AKA Sweet and High.

EXIT

Important: Exit by climbing up your run and skiing the access ridge back to Buttermilk. If you continue through the forest below the obvious bowls, you can become lost in confusing, wooded terrain (several rescues have occurred here), or end up suffering a lengthy ski back to West Buttermilk along the Government Trail hiking route.

Before uphilling, check Buttermilk's uphill ski policy and instructions.

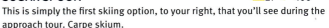

1 SUGAR SPOON — 27° 400'

This is simply the first skiing option, to your right, that you'll see during the approach tour. Carpe skium.

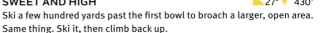

2 SWEET AND HIGH — 27° 430'

Ski a few hundred yards past the first bowl to broach a larger, open area. Same thing. Ski it, then climb back up.

To McNamara Hut
1

ATES 1

VAN HORN PARK ASPEN

The town of Aspen is nestled in the heart of Colorado's steep Elk Mountains. Hence, terrain with minimal avalanche danger is difficult to find. One solution is to head north of the town to an area of lower-elevation "foothill" mountains, where the original huts and trails of the 10th Mountain Division Hut Association were established. Because "hutzers" use this route to access the 10th Mountain McNamara Hut, you may see quite a few other skiers, often with large packs brimming with adult beverages. When the hut skiers see your wine and cheese spread at Van Horn, they might stop and share. You never know.

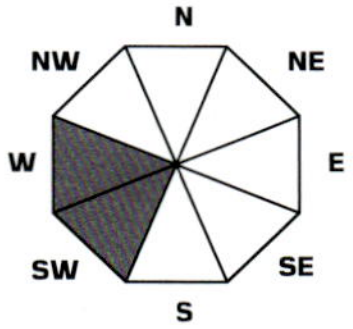

This route completely avoids avalanche terrain.

Lower Trailhead: From the town of Aspen, drive Main Street to Mill Street (stoplight intersection near the center of town, next to the Hotel Jerome). Turn north on Mill and drive a short distance down a hill, then 0.25 miles across a bridge over the Roaring Fork River. Bear left after the bridge and follow Red Mountain Road for 1.2 miles to its second switchback. Just before the switchback, turn right and downhill on Hunter Creek Road. Drive approximately 0.5 miles on Hunter Creek Road, then take a hard left on an unpaved driveway leading up past a water tank and utility building 300' to the lower trailhead parking area.

Upper Trailhead: With limited parking that's almost always filled, this trailhead is used more as a drop-off or walk-to destination from the Lower Trailhead. Walking roads in your ski boots, with your skis strapped to your pack, is not optimal; we thus recommend engaging a friend or taxi. Follow directions above to the Lower Trailhead parking driveway. Continue past the driveway northeast on the Hunter Creek Road through a pair of short stone pillars. Follow Hunter Creek Road for 0.7 miles to a three-way intersection. Take a hard right turn, and continue east 0.10 miles through two sharp switchbacks. Continue up the road following signs and avoiding private property. You'll eventually reach the well-signed parking area in the Hunter Creek valley. GPS is mandatory for newcomers seeking this trailhead. Taxi drivers may know it, but don't count on it. As of this printing, a taxi costs about $20, including tip.

The Van Horn Park tour follows old, well-defined logging roads and is marked with signs and the 10th Mountain hut system's blue plastic diamonds. There are, however, several confusing junctions where newcomers can make good use of GPS. Begin with climbing skins (though you may first do some dirt-walking on south facing hillside roads). From the tiny parking area at Upper Hunter Creek trailhead, head north up an obvious road which soon swings east and climbs the side of the valley. Bear right at the first somewhat obvious Y-intersection (about 1.3 miles from the trailhead). You'll soon reach a large clearing known as Lower Van Horn Park. Continue easterly to reach Van Horn Park. Ski easterly up the north side of Van Horn Park to Lower Van Horn Saddle (just a low-angled shelf) at 9,760'. Continue along the north side of the park to Upper Van Horn Park, then Upper Van Horn Saddle, a more definitive saddle at 9,925'.

EXIT

Reverse the access trail and snow-covered road. It is all low-angle and can be a nice cruise. Though you might find it especially quick during icy conditions (to put it nicely).

1 VAN HORN DESCENT

22° 430'

Ski the general line of your ascent through the tilted meadows, or explore northwesterly-facing terrain to climbers' right, where you might find better powder.

Grizzly Peak
INDEPENDENCE PASS SOUTH SIDE
15.1
3
4
1
2
HWY 82
P
Independence Pass North
(next page)

ATES 1

INDEPENDENCE PASS SOUTH SIDE

In spring, usually by Memorial Day weekend or soon after, CDOT completes their snow removal work on Independence Pass. Opening “The Pass” is cause for celebration among Colorado ski mountaineers, because the pass road provides access to about 200 square miles of beautiful alpine touring terrain. In winter, the closed, snow-covered road is a popular snowmobile and dog-walking route, and thus is not recommended as a moderate ski tour in and of itself.

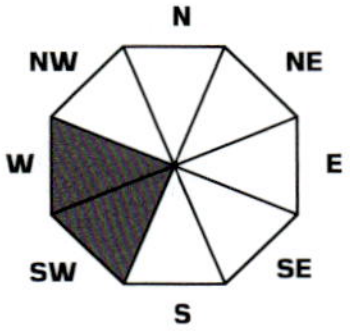

While much of the ski touring available from Independence Pass involves avalanche terrain, several routes near the pass summit parking are lower-angled. Because of the prevalent avalanche terrain and difficult access, the area is not recommended for winter skiing. Instead, enjoy during spring mornings after the road opens, when the snowpack is compacted and solidified, providing a “corn snow” surface and lower likelihood of avalanches. If you do use the road as a ski tour, know it is exposed to numerous avalanche paths.

Drive Colorado Hwy. 82 from I-70 (Glenwood Springs), or from Hwy. 24 (east side). The Independence Pass summit is obvious.

These tours begin at the Independence Pass summit parking area. The traditional approach is to ski southeast across a lengthy flat area, then continue southeast to the summit of Heart Attack Hill. If you’re here during a spring morning, you’ll notice skiers continuing higher on a ridge to the south. This is Snow Fence Ridge, which accesses advanced avalanche-prone terrain such as Mountain Boy.

EXIT

All tours end on Hwy. 82. The light tours on the pass, which use Heart Attack Hill, bring you back to (or very near), the summit parking lot. Skiers enjoying 4th of July or Mountain Boy can either hitchhike to their parking or prevail upon a friend for a ride.

1 HEART ATTACK HILL

20° 400’

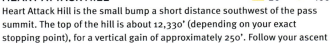

Heart Attack Hill is the small bump a short distance southwest of the pass summit. The top of the hill is about 12,330’ (depending on your exact stopping point), for a vertical gain of approximately 250’. Follow your ascent route back to the parking area.

2 CARDIAC RUN

22° 500’

From the top of Heart Attack Hill, point your descent northerly to the road below, instead of easterly back to the parking area. You’ll extend your vertical loss by about 100’ and find a much better ski pitch. This is a terrific place for never-evers to learn ski touring techniques. Do not drop to the west (towards Aspen) down steeper, avalanche-prone slopes. Walk the road back to the pass summit, or skin Heart Attack again, then ski east to the pass summit.

3 MOUNTAIN BOY

38° 870’

While this is avalanche terrain—not a low-angle tour—we include Mountain Boy and 4th of July Bowls in this guide for the sake of completeness, as they’re both popular after Hwy. 82 opens. Springtime avalanche danger is easier to predict and avoid than that of winter, but if you’re not trained in snowpack assessment, stick to runs 1 and 2 and ski during morning hours after a cool night. All Mountain Boy tours end near the second tight switchback on the easterly side of the pass.

4 4TH OF JULY BOWLS

45° 1,590’

These steep, avalanche-prone bowls drop northerly to Hwy. 82. Ski them only during the firm, stable spring snow conditions you usually find during morning hours after a cool, clear night. Access by skiing west past Heart Attack Hill.

Round-trip: 0.75 mi

15.2 INDEPENDENCE PASS NORTH SIDE

ATES 1

INDEPENDENCE PASS NORTH SIDE

For general information about Independence Pass, refer to the previous page.

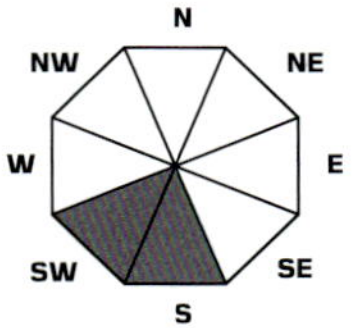

This side of Independence becomes more advanced and complex the farther you get from the road.To keep it light and simple, stick to the slopes adjacent to the pass summit.

Drive Colorado Hwy. 82 from I-70 (Glenwood Springs), or from Hwy. 24 (east side). The Independence Pass summit is obvious. Be there early to avoid parking challenges.

Blue Peak Approach: Walk across Hwy. 82 and begin. You're above timberline, so navigation is somewhat easy. But don't let down your guard; know where you're going and have a plan. Climb northerly for 0.5 miles, swing around the west side of Blarney Peak, then make a pleasant, mostly low-angled climb to the lower flanks of the south face of Blue. For more challenging avalanche terrain navigation, continue up to the summit of Blue. This south face of Blue Peak just reaches 32° slope angles.
Blarney Peak Approach: Walk across Hwy. 82 and begin. Climb due north for 0.4 miles, then follow Blarney's ridge northeast all the way to the summit. This ridge is not always covered in snow, so don't expect glorious pow turns.
Lower Blarney Approach: Walk across Hwy. 82 and begin. Climb and contour northeast into the lower south bowl of Blarney Peak. There is overhead avalanche exposure here, so if avalanche conditions exist, avoid this route.

EXIT

All our Indy North Side tours return to Hwy. 82, most often to the summit parking lot via your approach route. You'll notice that skiers often descend the lower reaches of Blue Peak westerly to a lower parking area on Hwy. 82. Only explore this option once you're familiar with the area.

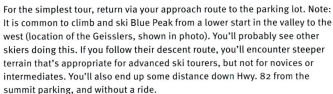

1 LOWER BLUE PEAK — 27° 900'

For the simplest tour, return via your approach route to the parking lot. Note: It is common to climb and ski Blue Peak from a lower start in the valley to the west (location of the Geisslers, shown in photo). You'll probably see other skiers doing this. If you follow their descent route, you'll encounter steeper terrain that's appropriate for advanced ski tourers, but not for novices or intermediates. You'll also end up some distance down Hwy. 82 from the summit parking, and without a ride.

2 BLARNEY PEAK — 29° 1,400'

From the summit (or from the end of the snow patches), descend the approach route along the ridge. Once you're off the ridge, aim for the pass summit parking lot. As you ski, beware of cornices you observed during the ascent.

3 LOWER BLARNEY — 29° 400'

This route offers minimal vertical. Do several laps if you're looking for a workout. Enjoy open, low-angled terrain with many obvious options. You may experience the legendary Rocky Mountain high while making turns off the Continental Divide; enjoy, but don't let your exuberance take you down so low that walking up the road to the parking area is a Rocky Mountain bummer (though hitchhiking is possible).

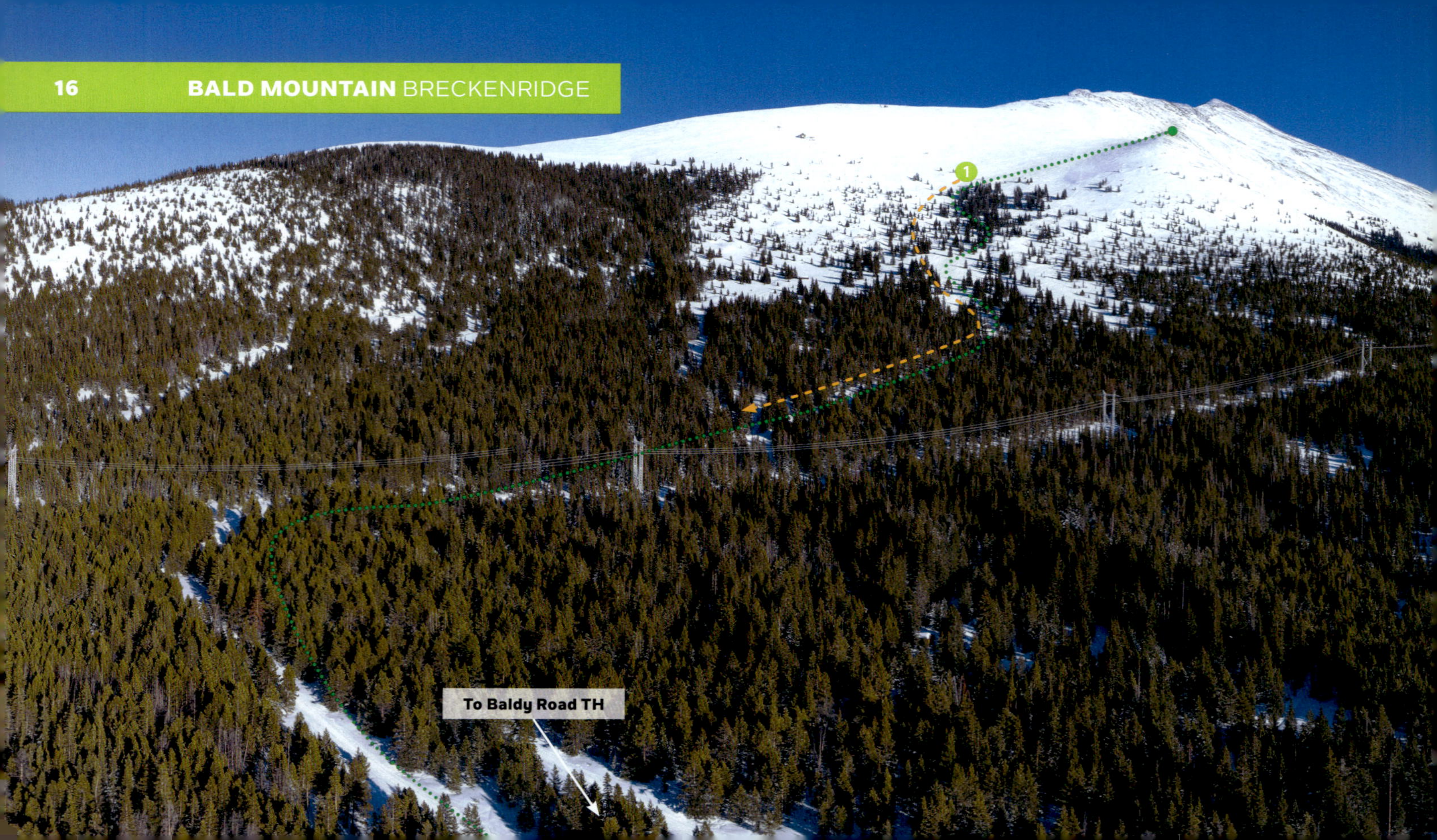
16
BALD MOUNTAIN BRECKENRIDGE
1
To Baldy Road TH

ATES 1

BALD MOUNTAIN BRECKENRIDGE

Locally known as "Baldy," here's yet another creatively named Colorado peak. Levity aside, this aspect of Bald Mountain provides one of Colorado's best areas of low-angle alpine skiing terrain. It's thus one of our favorite tours.

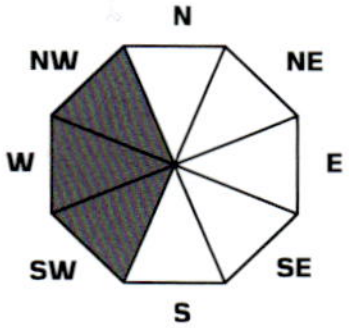

Reduced slope angle is your friend. Plenty of steep, avalanche-prone terrain exists in this area, but it's easy to avoid. The terrain steepens above timberline. While unusual, large avalanches could thus threaten from above. As with most of our suggested areas, be extra conservative when avalanche danger is forecasted as Considerable or High. In that case, the snow-covered approach road is a pleasant walk with a glide return.

GPS is mandatory for the latter portion of this complex trailhead drive, but must be activated only when you're on the south side of the town of Breckenridge; otherwise, the artificial unintelligence may direct you through a maze of residential roads, or worse. As of this writing, entering "Emmit Lode bus stop" into Google Maps led to the trailhead.

Drive I-70 and turn off at either of two exits for Frisco. From Frisco, drive Hwy. 9 about 10 miles to Breckenridge. Stay on Hwy. 9 as it bends south through Breckenridge, then blends with South Main Street. About 11 miles south of Frisco, take a left off Hwy. 9/South-Main onto the Boreas Pass Road (County Road 10). Drive a mile to an intersection and take a left to stay on the Boreas Pass Road. Follow Boreas Pass Road for 0.8 miles and turn left onto Mt. Baldy Road. Continue 1.3 miles to the trailhead parking and signboard. To save your sanity, and the planet, we recommend reaching this trailhead via municipal bus. To do so, follow Hwy. 9 to the Gondola Parking Lot and proximate Breckenridge Bus Station. Catch the Boreas Loop bus to the Emmit Lode stop.

From the trailhead, follow the snow-covered and normally well-beaten Mt. Baldy 4x4 road. At 0.8 miles, stay left at a fork. At 1.3 miles, you'll reach the Iowa Mill buildings. The skintrack leaves the road at the mill and climbs the fall line to timberline. It continues up the fall line to crest a ridge, then swings right to The Nipple.

EXIT

Return to the Baldy Trailhead via the approach road. After you make a few speed-control turns just below the mill, the angle lessens to a glide with two short sections of skating. When skiing the terrain above Iowa Mill, take care to pick up the road at the mill. The vast forests below the mill are a good place to become lost, or deviated so far from the trailhead you'll need hours to find your way back.

1 BALDY DESCENT

29° 1,390'

To keep it light, turn around at timberline and ski back to Iowa Mill. If you continue above timberline to The Nipple, ski lower-angled terrain off The Nipple that follows the general route of the skintrack. Avoid steeper terrain.

Round-trip: 5 mi

2
1
P
To Breckendrige

ATES 1

HOOSIER PASS NORTHSTAR

This route from Hoosier Pass is somewhat straightforward, as it follows low-angle slopes and a defined ridgeline above timberline. You pay a price, however, as the area is only safe during good weather, and ideally in springtime during the snowpack melt-freeze cycle. The reward is an incredible view of several fourteeners.

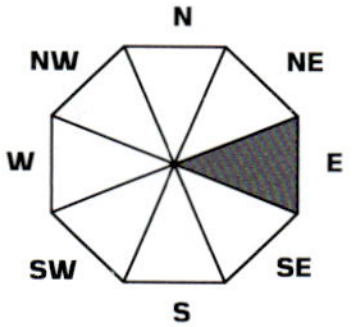

On the Quick Shot route, notice the small rollover at 11,900' in the middle of the slope that tips up to 35° for about 50 vertical feet. This is the only part of this slope that is over 30°. If you choose to explore farther up the ridge of Northstar Mountain, staying on the ridge will avoid steep slopes for up to 2.5 miles to 13,400'. As with most mountain ridges, terrain to either side may be highly avalanche-prone; it is imperative to descend your avalanche-safe ascent route. Do not drop off the sides of the ridge! The complete ridge tour is only recommended for experts, as there are many places where a small mistake can place you in peril.

Drive Hwy. 9 to the Hoosier Pass summit. Trailhead signs and parking on the west side of the road make the trailhead obvious. Hwy. 9 is maintained all year with occasional closures for weather and avalanche mitigation. Space can be limited during a sunny weekend day. Park wisely and with respect.

From the trailhead parking at Hoosier Pass (11,500'), simply ski west up obvious low angled glades. Gain the Northstar Ridge after about 0.25 miles. This is your turnaround point for the "light" tour. Experts may continue on Northstar Ridge.

EXIT

Return to parking via your ascent route.

1 HOOSIER QUICK SHOT — 28° — 275'

Return to the parking lot via your approach route.

2 NORTHSTAR RIDGE — 30° — 2,200'

From the summit of Northstar Mountain, or from anywhere else on the ridge, descend your ascent route to the pass summit parking lot.

Dyer Mountain
Mount Sherman
Ball Mountain
2
1
P

ATES 1

BALL MOUNTAIN LEADVILLE

Sweeping low-angle peaks, incredible views, and abandoned mines make Ball Mountain a classic Leadville tour. It's a short drive from the town of Leadville to the trailhead, or you can extend your tour by starting in town on the extensive "Mineral Belt Trail," a circuitous network of groomed nordic trails. Advanced route-finding and avalanche terrain knowledge skills can help you lengthen this tour up and along the ridge connecting East Ball Mountain and West Dyer Mountain, thus making a large loop around South Evans Gulch.

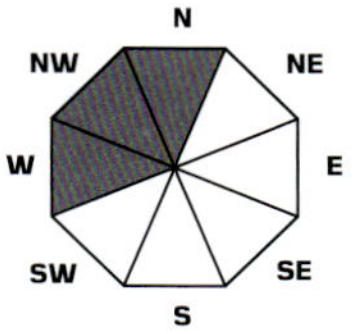

You can avoid avalanche terrain by staying on the west aspect of Ball Mountain. Be cautious of the northwest-facing bowl; it can be a fun descent, but it tilts to 35°. Near the trailhead, be mindful of the small, steep slopes that flank parts of the road.

From Leadville, drive up East 7th Street for 2.5 miles, leaving town and entering Evans Gulch. Park at the most appropriate spot near the snowplow turnaround, at about 2.5 miles. Maintenance and plowing depend on the amount of snow falling (or blowing) in the area. East 7th Street is usually plowed at least 2.5 miles from downtown Leadville. The parking is free, but limited. When deciding where to park, do your best to not block access for plows and other vehicles.

Begin by climbing the road until you see a low-angle route option, gaining the west ridge of Ball Mountain. Often, you can do this by following the various mining roads until you reach CR-1 (also an extension of 5th Street). Once you're on the flats below West Bowl, point southeast to gain the upper west ridge to Ball's summit. End at the summit and pick your descent.

EXIT

These runs take you back to Evans basin and back to the parking lot—so long as you follow the main drainage.

1 WEST BOWL

28° 1,350'

From the summit, head west and descend any part of the face.

2 EAST RIDGE

29° 1,350'

From the summit, point your sticks east towards the saddle that separates Ball from West Dyer. At the saddle, head north through the gulch, which eventually drains you back to the bottom of Evans Gulch.

East Side grooming report: The local nordic grooming report might help you decide where you will park and if you can use the east side trails to approach Ball Mountain.

Round-trip: 2 mi

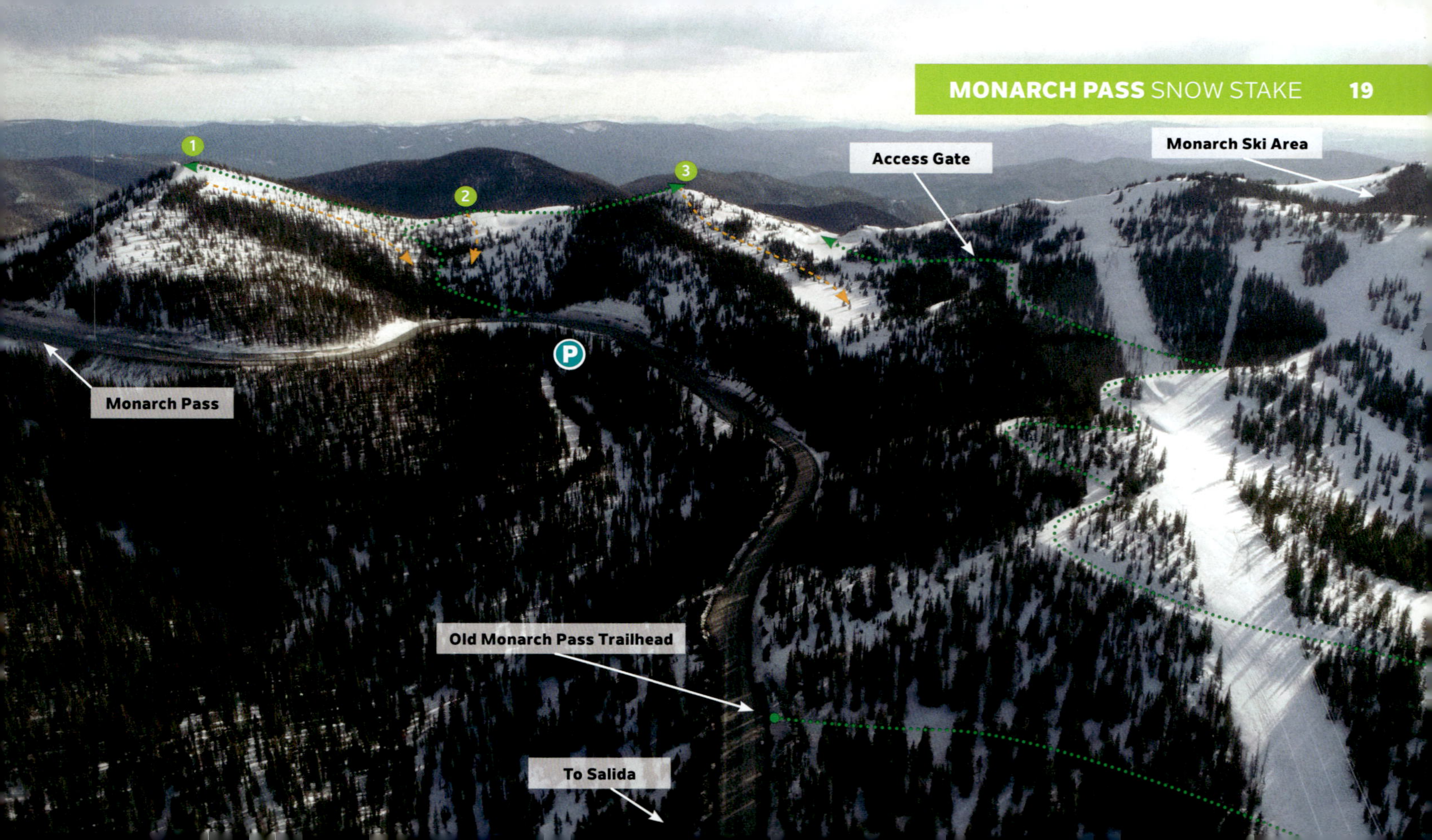
Monarch Ski Area
Access Gate
1
2
3
P
Monarch Pass
Old Monarch Pass Trailhead
To Salida

ATES 1

MONARCH PASS SNOW STAKE

Monarch Pass provides a wealth of ski touring with manageable avalanche hazard. With a Monarch Mountain uphill or lift pass, you can also access this terrain from the ski area. Likewise, you can enter the ski area from the backcountry through any one of their access gates. These runs are short, sweet, lower-angle glades, somewhat protected from snow-damaging wind.

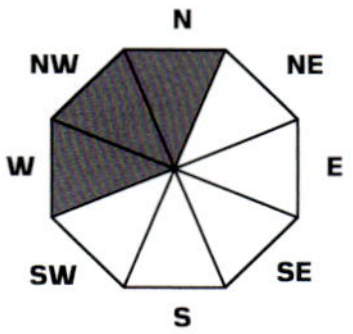

Do not ski this area during higher avalanche danger forecasts. Occasional rollovers can be found in these slopes, so learn to identify and avoid them.

Park in the large plowed area on the east side of the road 0.5 miles from Monarch Pass. From the parking area, cross the road (south). This is a popular parking lot; please park head-in (not parallel) and close to your neighbor. If you park at the Old Monarch Pass TH just a few hundred yards down the highway, heed the same parking advice.

Snow Stake Approach from Snow Stake Parking: Ascend climber's right up a gully leading to a bowl. Aim for the obvious saddle 0.5 miles ahead, between the two round summits. Turn around here and pick your downhill route. Or extend your tour northwest along the Continental Divide to Old Monarch Pass, or to the ski resort (if entering the resort from the backcountry, acquire an uphill pass before your tour).
Old Monarch Approach: You can also reach this area by climbing up Old Monarch Pass road (consult a map or GPS). This TH is 0.5 miles north down Hwy. 50. To keep it ultra-mellow, ski down the old road.
Monarch Ski Area Approach: The third way to reach this zone is by climbing up Monarch Mountain. Uphill route information is available when you acquire your uphill pass, or from the ski area website.
See photo on page 80.

EXIT

Stay on the north side of the Continental Divide and descend to HWY 50.

1 SNOW STAKE — 28° 440'

This is the peak directly above Monarch Pass. It hosts mellow glades that drop you back to the highway. Climb this peak via the Snow Stake Approach, or the resort's access gate (see photo), then along the ridgeline. Descend north through the glades. If you point your skis anywhere but north (back to the parking lot), you may be on slopes greater than 30°. Regarding all the routes described here, people will often be skiing above and below you. Travel with respect.

2 SHORT STAKE — 26° 350'

Another short run for quick laps. A nice way to ski this route is to access it from the ski area, or from Old Monarch Road. In that case, descend the glades to the highway and skin back up to Snow Stake.

3 ROAD RUN — 20° 350'

A short and very low-angle run. For turns here, you'll need a springtime corn crust; otherwise, you'll find yourself striding downhill. Do multiple laps using the often pre-established skintrack, or traverse to the Old Monarch Pass road for more laps.

20 SNODGRASS FRONT SIDE CRESTED BUTTE

ATES 1

SNODGRASS FRONT SIDE CRESTED BUTTE

Snodgrass Mountain is the place to play within a stone's throw of Crested Butte Mountain Resort. The snow-covered road to the summit is usually groomed, and almost always tracked with constant foot/ski/snowshoe traffic. The road provides an avalanche safe route. Removing your skins at the summit and zooming back down the road is fun by itself. Or enjoy the lower-angled options we describe here. Conditions are most enjoyable when the air is cold, and a few fresh inches of powder lay over a solid base.

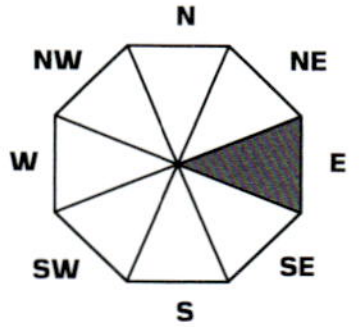

Tip: Our atlas and topo map *Backcountry Skiing: Crested Butte, Colorado* details many other routes in the Snodgrass area.

The road to the summit entirely avoids avalanche terrain. Unless you follow the prescribed "Front Side" run, understand that leaving the road can bring you into confusing and complicated terrain with many rollovers, terrain traps, and an infamously shallow snowpack.

From Crested Butte: Drive north on Gothic Road (317) for 4.5 miles. Gothic Road is maintained to the top of the road's descent into the East River Valley. You'll see a bus stop on the west side and the ski resort's maintenance building on the east side. The designated parking area is free and often crowded. The Snodgrass trailhead serves a network of Nordic trails, recreation on Snodgrass Mountain, and is the trailhead for a 3.7-mile trek to the town of Gothic.

Climb west from the parking area towards a fenced-in pond and continue west on the groomed snow road. Skiers often create shortcuts between road switchbacks. If in doubt, stick to the road. The skintrack (and road) end at the mountain's round, timbered summit.

EXIT

The easiest and most straightforward exit follows the approach road back to the parking lot.

1 FRONT SIDE

26° 1,540'

This run adds fun and adventure to the common descent down the road. Follow the route shown in the photo, while looking for your own small stashes of powder just off of the road. As you descend, your first opportunity is as the road takes a sharp left (north) turn to wrap around the mountain. Descend east, off of the road, down to a large meadow below. Once in the meadow, regain the road and follow it for about 300 yards to a sharp left (north) turn. Leave the road again and descend the gentle slope to your right. Regain the road and head southeast until you reach the top of the hill from where you can see the parking area. Here, you can find more low-angle turns by descending skier's right of the road.

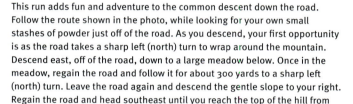

Baldy Cinco
Baldy No Es Cinco
Snow Mesa
1
2
To Lake City
P
To Creede

ATES 1

SPRING CREEK PASS BALDY CINCO

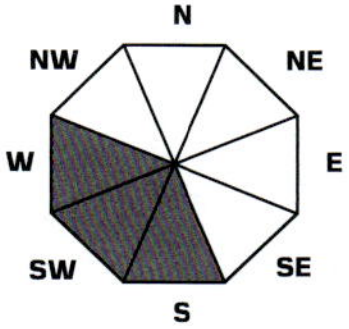

Baldy Cinco is out there. In a snowstorm, this tour will have you feeling like you landed on a cross-continental journey in Antarctica. But on a splitter bluebird Colorado day, you'll count this as one of the best light tours in the state. Located between Lake City and Creede, this Continental Divide Trail (CDT) tour brings you across a bizarre mesa and a big peak summit. The reward is a 360° panorama of the San Juan and La Garita mountains, and many fourteeners.

As with many of the routes in this book, it is wise to avoid this terrain during Considerable and High danger days. As you ascend above timberline, be aware of a steep slope above you, to climber's right. To reach the mesa without traveling beneath this slope, make a switchback through the trees, north to climber's left, and gain the ridge and mesa this way. This ridge route, shown in red on our photo, avoids the small steep slope in the upper gully. If you are unable to assess conditions, timberline is a good place to turn around for a Glades lap.

From Lake City, drive south on Hwy. 149 over Slumgullion Pass to Spring Creek Pass. The parking area is on the west side of the highway at the pass summit. If the off-highway parking lot is plowed, that's the best place to park. Walk across the highway to begin the tour.

Begin by climbing east from the highway on an old road-cut through light timber, to climber's right of the official Continental Divide Trail. When you break timberline, it's time for some decisions (read the avalanche terrain notes above). When you reach Snow Mesa and begin trending slightly northwest along the CDT, aim for the saddle between Baldy Cinco (climber's right) and Baldy No Es Cinco (climber's left). The saddle is a nice turnaround point if you're not in need of a summit. To summit either peak, ascend from the saddle. Southern exposure and fierce winds can leave these ridges without snow. During an average snow season, you can usually ski to the top before April.

EXIT Return via your approach route by traversing west by southwest along Snow Mesa to Snow Mesa Glades. The glades bring you back to the highway, close to where you began skinning.

1 CINCO SADDLE — 28° — 2,510'

Descend via the approach route. The entire bowl between Cinco and No Es Cinco is skiable. All south faces from the summits are less than 30°. The north faces are steep descents through avalanche terrain that drop you into a different drainage, so keep it light by returning via your approach.

2 SNOW MESA GLADES — 28° — 1,200'

For the lightest tour from Spring Creek Pass, stay below timberline. These glades catch a lot of snow-damaging western sun, but after a storm, they can provide excellent low-angle powder laps. They're a pleasant way to finish the Baldy Cinco tour, or if visibility is bad, lap them all day. From timberline, stay close to the CDT and road-cut to avoid the steeper gully on skier's left.

22.1 RED MOUNTAIN PASS McMILLAN PEAK
1
US Basin

ATES 1

RED MOUNTAIN PASS McMILLAN PEAK

A San Juan "super tour." From the top of Red Mountain Pass, you can ski to a summit, then return via low-angle terrain. This zone is often beaten down by wind and sun, making it a potentially challenging descent in terms of snow conditions. Still, when the pow is fine or the corn is ripe, this is a fantastic high-alpine run with some of the best views in the Juans. Note this tour yields a good view of the West Side Mini Golf area (next page). Much of the text in the next two pages is sourced and revised from Beacon Guidebooks' *Backcountry Skiing: Silverton, Colorado* with the permission of author Josh Kling. We thank Josh for helping keep our information consistent and accurate.

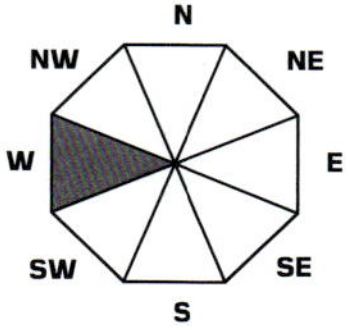

As mentioned above, this zone can be traveled as low-angle, lower-risk terrain. However, there is plenty of avalanche terrain in the area. Because of the complicated nature of the McMillan terrain, this is a good place to practice route-finding skills by taking your time, studying slope-angle maps, and discussing the different slopes you see as you tour. As with most of our suggested areas, be extra conservative when avalanche danger is rated Considerable or High.

From Durango and Silverton: Drive north on Hwy. 550 to the summit of Red Mountain Pass. There is a large parking area on the east side of the highway. Be sure to park at least three feet from the white shoulder line, and be aware this is a heavily used, often crowded trailhead.

Follow the unmaintained road grade, CR 14, east towards McMillan Peak. After 0.75 miles, tour east up the west ridge of McMillan.

EXIT

Runs within this photo bring you back to the trailhead or just to the south. The sprawling terrain can be confusing, especially in storm conditions. Stay keen—and seriously, enable your GPS and carry a good map!

1 McMILLAN WEST RIDGE

28° 1,700'

Descend your ascent route west from the summit. There are many terrain features to play on and explore. Use your slope angle meter and practice safe route-finding.

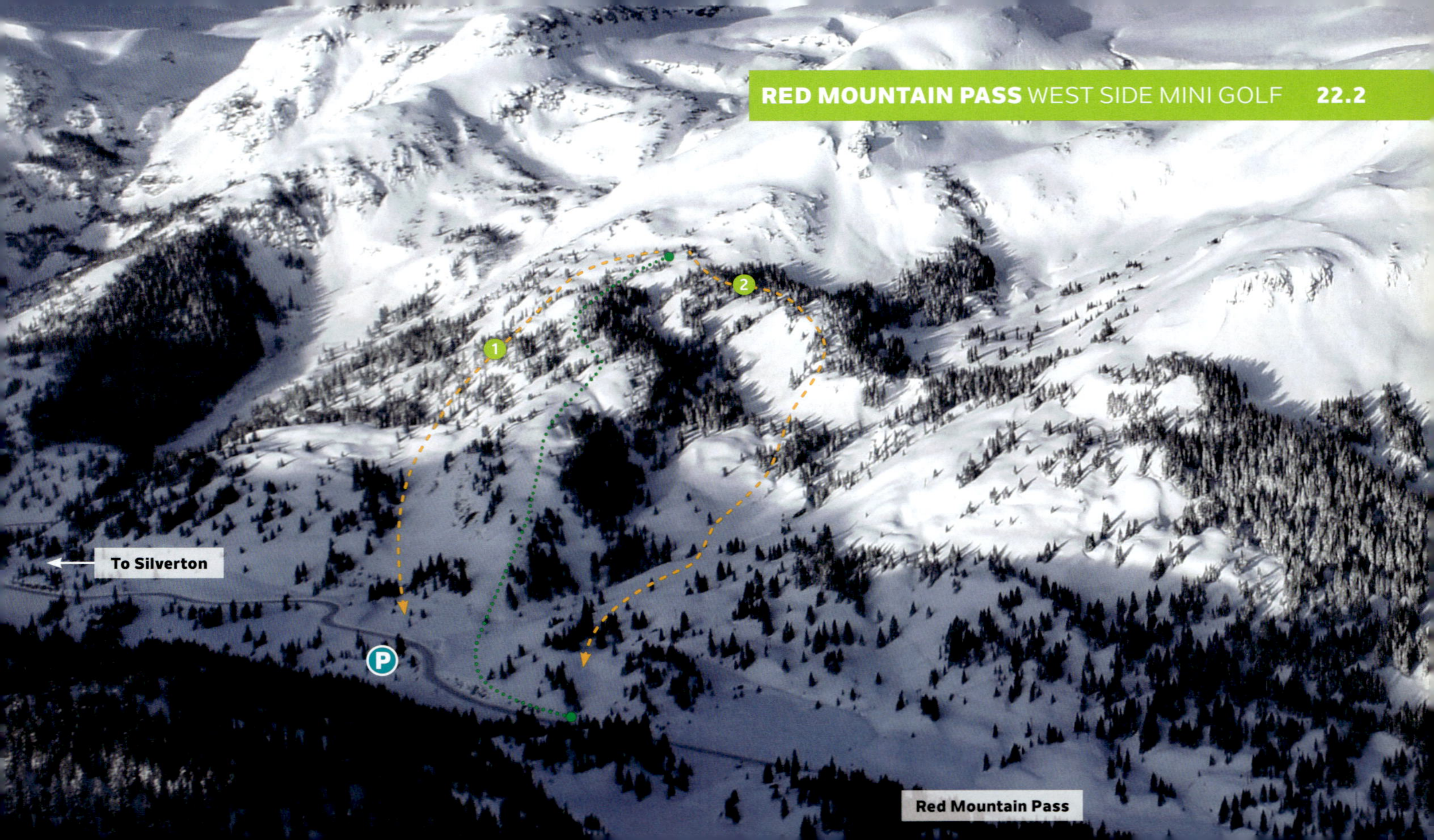
RED MOUNTAIN PASS WEST SIDE MINI GOLF 22.2
1
2
To Silverton
P
Red Mountain Pass

ATES 1

RED MOUNTAIN PASS WEST SIDE MINI GOLF

Also referred to as Telephone Pole Ridge, the west side of Red Mountain Pass has numerous "mini-golf" tours suitable for a novice backcountry skier who just completed their first Recreational Level 1 avalanche course. The west side provides lots of room for creativity, with no single option for the up or the down.

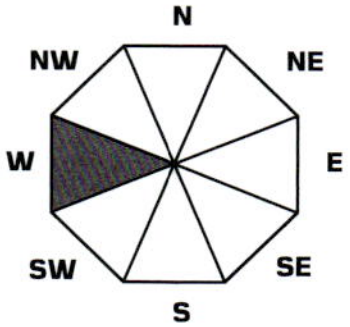

While these tours tend to stick to smaller, less consequential terrain, they are all within or near avalanche terrain. For safe skiing in this area, exercise proper precautions and terrain assessment. To do so, you must have at least intermediate-level avalanche safety skills.

From Durango and Silverton: Drive north on Hwy. 550 to the summit of Red Mountain Pass. The best parking for Telephone Pole Ridge is 0.3 miles north of the Addie S Cabin and 0.3 miles south of the top of the pass on the west side of the road. If this parking is full or otherwise unusable, park at the pass summit and tour the road bank to the base of Telephone Pole Ridge.

This is the common approach track for the short shots just off the highway. It is a snow-covered road. Numerous ascent options access these shorter tours. Telephone Pole Ridge is a good choice if you're not sure where to go.

EXIT

The runs described here drop you to the highway. You may have to walk alongside the road to return to your vehicle.

1 FRONT YARD 28° 650'

Descend to the highway via skier's right of your approach track.

2 LOWER SUNNY BUMPS 28° 650'

As above, stay to the far skier's left of the approach track.

Alberta's Cousin
1
Wolf Creek Ski Area
P

ATES 1

WOLF CREEK PASS ALBERTA'S COUSIN

Wolf Creek Pass is above average. Winter storms can be apocalyptic, the snowpack depth often exceeds statewide averages, and navigation isn't always easy. Much of Wolf Creek's backcountry is committing and steep. Yet simple, lower-angle options exist. Enjoy the tours detailed below as a fine introduction to this unique place.

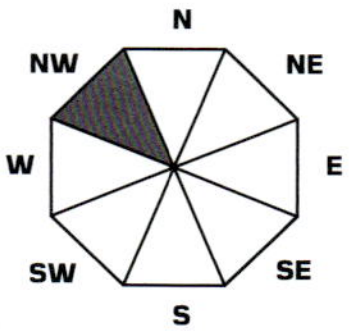

This route does not cross avalanche terrain. Note that the southeast aspect of Alberta's Cousin is an avalanche path that crosses Hwy. 160 over an avalanche tunnel.

Park in the large plowed lot on the north side of the highway, 0.25 miles east of the Wolf Creek Pass summit sign. This is a better starting point than the summit parking lot.

Ascend south from the parking lot. Skin 0.5 miles up a low-angle gully to a large meadow crossed by a powerline. Just before you pass under the powerline, turn sharply right and ascend southeast for about 0.5 miles to the treeless summit. Turn around to keep it light.

EXIT

From the meadow at the bottom of Alberta's Cousin Glades, return to the parking lot via your ascent route through the gully and trees. Do not be lured by ski tracks heading south and east from the summit. Descending east or south will put you in steep avalanche terrain that drops you 3 miles from the parking area.

1 ALBERTA'S COUSIN GLADES — 18° — 320'

Descend northwest, parallel to the approach route. Enjoy the perfectly spaced trees as you explore all flanks of this northwest aspect. The slope angles here are quite relaxed—you'll be shuffling your skis both uphill and down if the snow is deep. Moreover, the vertical loss is minimal, so consider linking this tour with Lobo *(next page)*.

Round-trip: 2.5 mi

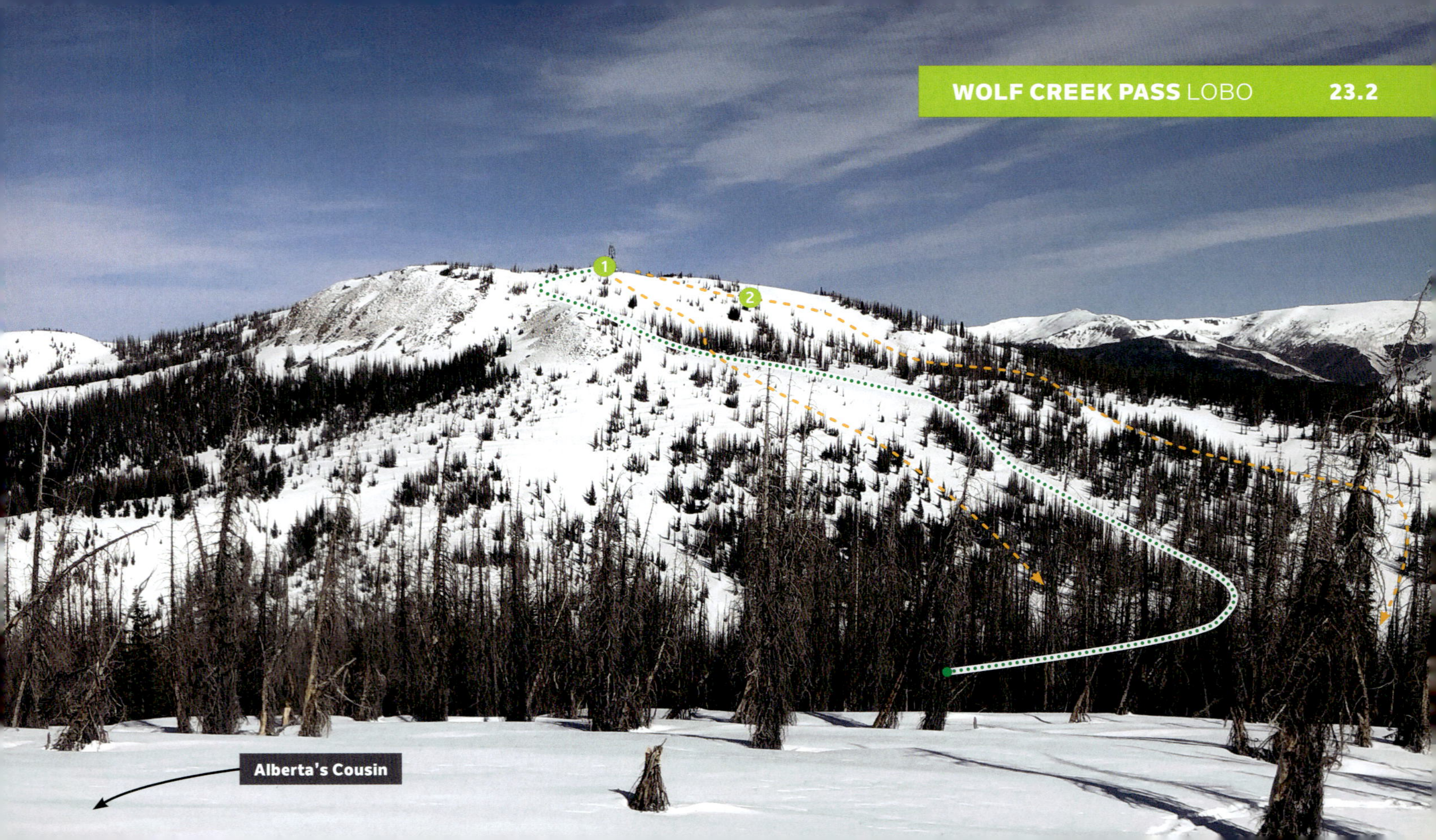
1
2
Alberta's Cousin

ATES 1

WOLF CREEK PASS LOBO

Ski up and soak in some classic southwest views, including an excellent vantage of the Wolf Creek Ski Area, before you head down to Pagosa for a soak in the hot springs.

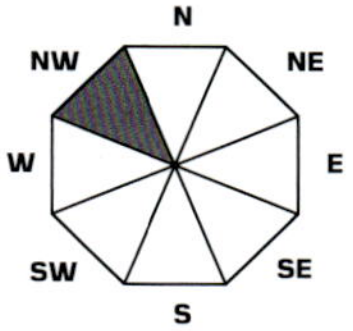

Lobo has plenty of steeper pitches. This route keeps the angles low and does not cross avalanche terrain, but it does get close. Take care not to stray.

Park in the large, plowed lot on the north side of the highway, 0.25 miles east of the Wolf Creek Pass summit sign. This is a better starting point than the summit parking lot.

Ascend south from the parking lot. Skin 0.5 miles up a low-angle gully, to a large meadow crossed by a powerline. Just before you cross under the powerline, take a sharp left turn and ascend westerly for another 0.5 miles to the Lobo Overlook summit. Descend from here.

EXIT

From the meadow at the bottom of Lobo and Alberta's Glades, return to the parking lot via your ascent route through the gully and trees.

1 POWERLINE GLADES

25° 540'

Descend east along the gladed powerline path. This open run feels more like a timber-cut resort slope than a true backcountry line.

2 LOBO GLADES

28° 560'

Descend east to skier's right of the powerlines, gradually gaining more distance between your tracks and the Powerline Glades. This brings you back to the area where the approach route enters the big meadow.

RESORT UPHILLS

High avalanche danger. Brand new equipment. Teaching a newcomer. Training for a race. Spending low-stress time with friends and loved ones. There are so many good reasons to opt for uphill skiing at the resort. (Every so often, uphilling at sunrise even gets us "firsties" on a pow day.) In the remaining pages, we list some of the best Colorado resorts for uphilling, also known as "piste touring," and we provide their current policies and routes (as of the 20/21 season).

The Colorado ski resorts we cover below have maintained consistent uphill routes and policies over the past five to ten years. While we work hard to verify this information, it is your job to verify any resort's current uphill rules. As an uphill skier, you are a guest of these resorts. Please respect their policies, employees, and other patrons in order to keep our uphill privileges available.

During all uphill, travel I will:

- ✓ Check resort policies and terrain status.
- ✓ Abide by all resort policies, laws, and regulations.
- ✓ Stay to the side of runs.
- ✓ Wear clothing and lights that improve my visibility.
- ✓ Avoid areas where machinery is operating.
- ✓ Obey all dog regulations.
- ✓ Clean up after my dog, always.
- ✓ Be aware that resort EMS services are not available outside of operating hours.
- ✓ Not enter closed trails and terrain.

Uphill skiing equipment recommended checklist

- ✓ Skis/splitboard
- ✓ Boots/poles/skins
- ✓ Goggles (clear lenses for dawn and dusk sessions)
- ✓ Sunglasses (clear lenses for dawn and dusk sessions)
- ✓ Helmet
- ✓ Headlamp
- ✓ Small rear bicycle button light
- ✓ Buff or mask (for the cold wind—or a pandemic)
- ✓ Snacks and water
- ✓ Trail map
- ✓ Offline digital map (this whole atlas can be downloaded with the Rakkup app)
- ✓ Access pass, armband, or whatever is required by the resort

A note about headlamps:

At ski areas such as Crested Butte Mountain Resort, ski patrol requires that you wear a headlamp outside of operating hours and that it's switched on regardless of daylight quality. While it may seem silly at first, we believe this excellent policy goes a long way to preventing tragic accidents. We recommend you follow this "headlamp on" policy at all ski areas, even if they don't require it. Some skiers even wear small bike lights and reflective clothing; we advocate this as well. When you're zipping down the piste after sunset and you see one of these illuminated skiers, you'll both be thankful you remembered your lights.

ROCKY TALKIE
THE MOUNTAIN RADIO
RANGE
1-5 Miles in Mountains
Max FRS Power (2-watts)
COLD RESISTANT
3-5 Day Battery Life
Even at -20° F
VERSATILITY
Optional IP67
Hand Mic
ROCKY TALKIE
CH 128

Sunspot Mountaintop Lodge
The Gondola
Arrow Chairlift
Gemini Express

WINTER PARK RESORT

Base Elevation: 9,085'

Vertical Gain to Sunspot Lodge: 1,620'

With a friendly uphilling policy and a location somewhat close to Colorado's population centers, Winter Park is a good bet for ski resort uphilling. While an uphilling fee is required, as of 2021, Winter Park directed the bulk of funds received from the fee as a $40,000 donation to Grand County Search and Rescue.

Dogs? Never allowed on the ski trails during operating hours. Beginning an hour after the lifts close and ending an hour before the lifts open in the morning, dogs under voice control are allowed on ski trails. Remove all waste.

Uphill Pass Required? Yes.

Uphill Pass Information: Everyone, including season passholders, must pre-purchase a pass and armband online. Armbands can be picked up at outside ticket offices at the Winter Park or Mary Jane base after the resort opens for the season. Uphiller armbands must be visible at all times.

Access/Parking: Winter Park is located in northern Colorado on Hwy. 40 via a somewhat lengthy drive from just about anywhere else. Note that the famed Amtrak "Ski Train" runs to and from Denver on weekends—expensive but worth an occasional ride to make the day special. Follow parking signs and attendants. Your pre-purchased uphill pass is your parking pass. Allow time for a shuttle to the base of the hill.

Winter Park Uphill Policy

Winter Park Armband Purchase

All Hours During Winter Season: Uphill access is allowed on any trail open that day within the following territories:

- Winter Park: All trails
- Mary Jane: All trails except double black diamond extreme terrain and the Trestle, Runaway, Sluice Box, and Pine Cliffs trails
- Parsenn Bowl: Only Village Way or Parry's Peek, unless the Panoramic Express is open to the public; then all trails are available for uphill access
- Vasquez Ridge Territory: All trails

After the Resort Closes for the Season:

Use only the following trails: Lower Hughes, Hughes, Norwegian, Little Pierre, and Sleeper (in Mary Jane).

Dedicated Uphill Route?

No, though some runs are permanently closed to uphilling.

Recommended Route: The classic morning workout: Up Larry Sale to Village Way. Then take Cranmer around the northwest side of Sunspot Hill to the top. To extend your tour, consider continuing south along Whistlestop to the terminus of Super Gauge Express and Lunch Rock Restaurant.

Non-Designated Route: During non-operating winter hours (8:30 AM to 4:30 PM) you can use any of the open routes. Pay attention to signs and run closures.

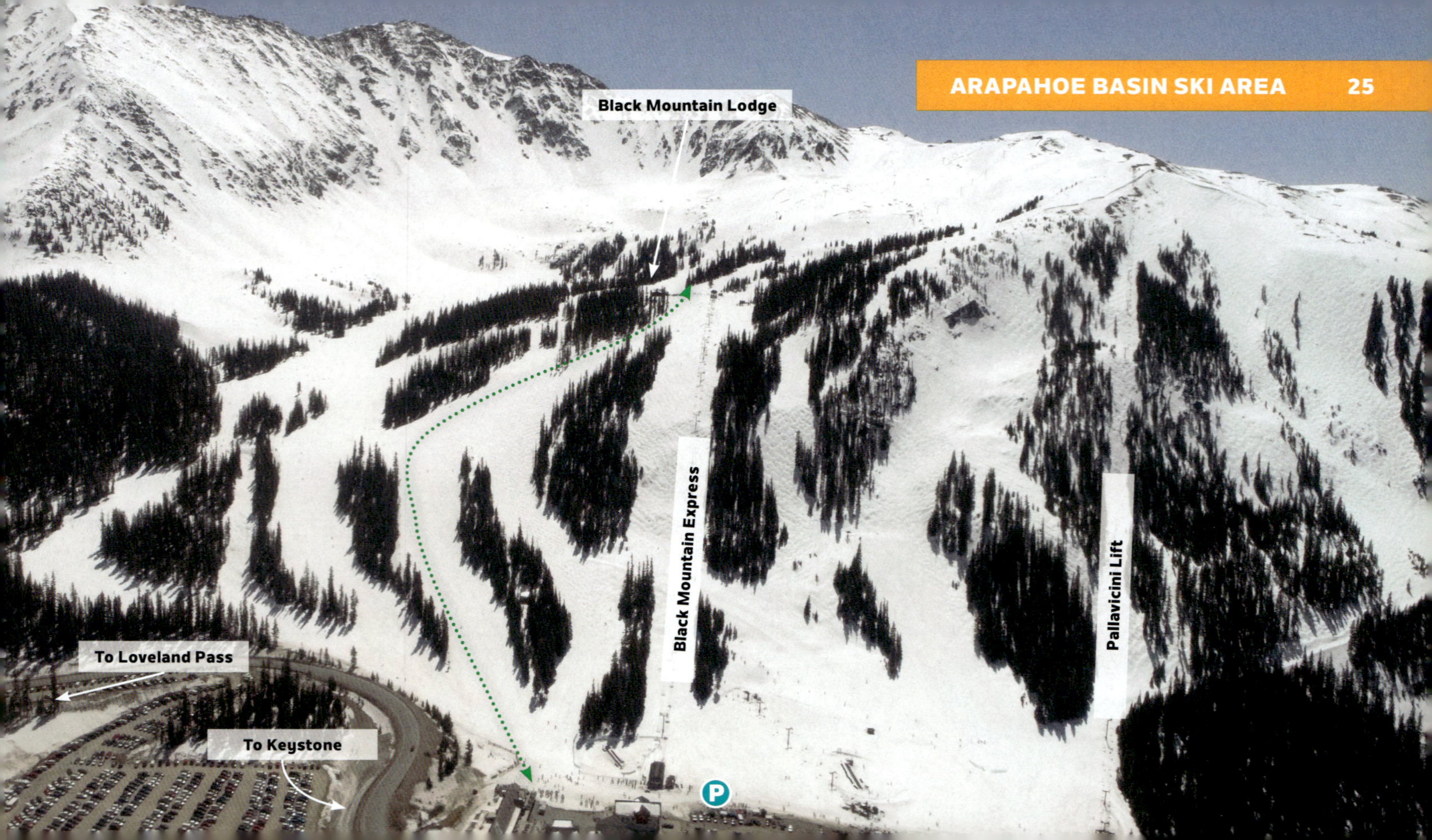
Black Mountain Lodge
Black Mountain Express
Pallavicini Lift
To Loveland Pass
To Keystone
P

ARAPAHOE BASIN SKI AREA

Base Elevation: 10,780'

Vertical Gain to Black Mountain Lodge: 720'

With their base area breaking timberline at 11,500 feet, Arapahoe Basin (A-Basin) boasts higher elevations than many other resorts. Consequently, they often win the early opening contest, as well as remaining open well into spring and sometimes summer. Thus, while winter weather at these elevations can make other venues more attractive for uphilling, you'll find excellent skiing during shoulder seasons, plenty of parking, and a pleasant "core" atmosphere.

Dogs?
Allowed only outside of operating hours and must be under control at all times. Remove all waste.

Uphill Pass Required? Yes.
Uphill Pass Information: Every uphiller (including A-Basin season passholders) must have an uphill access pass and an armband.

- The uphill pass is free to A-Basin season passholders. Reserve it online by logging into your account on the A-Basin e-store and signing the waiver.
- If you don't have an A-Basin season pass, you must purchase an uphill access pass online, and you must pick it up in person at their ticket windows, open 7 days per week from 8 AM to 4:30 PM.
- You must wear the provided armband while skinning or hiking, and carry your uphill access pass.
- The uphill access pass does not provide lift access.
- You cannot reuse a previous season's uphill pass. Please obtain a new one.

Access/Parking: Arapahoe Basin is located off I-70 on Hwy. 6. Uphill users who use the mountain during non-operating hours are asked to park in the Admin Lot (the small lot at the north end of the A-Frame) or in the parking area above the Admin Lot adjacent to Hwy. 6. The Early Riser, High Noon, and Last Chance lots are locked at 6 PM.

During Operating Hours: Uphill access is restricted to the eastern edge of High Noon between the Base Area and Black Mountain Lodge when lifts are turning. Do not ascend above the Black Mountain Lodge between the hours of 8:30 AM and 4:30 PM.
Non-Operating Hours: Uphill any of the open green and blue runs below mid-mountain/Black Mountain Lodge. Continue to the resort summit if desired.
All Hours: Do not enter closed terrain. Uphill access may be restricted for mountain operations or safety reasons. The East Wall, Beavers, and Steep Gullies, and all terrain parks, are closed to all users outside operating hours.

Dedicated Uphill Route?
Yes. Stick to the left (east) side of High Noon and below Black Mountain Lodge.
Designated Route: From the base area and ticket office, head southeast away from the Black Mountain Express lift. Ascend High Noon, looking for designated uphill route markers on the trees. Stay to the far climber's left (east) side of the High Noon run all the way to Black Mountain Lodge. The lodge is your turnaround point. Descend any open runs.
Non-Designated Route: Before and after winter operating hours (8:30 AM to 4:30 PM), you can use any of the open green and blue runs. Pay attention to signs and run closures.

Arapahoe Basin Terrain Status

Arapahoe Basin Uphill Information

Peak 10
Peak 9
Vista Haus
5 Chair
Rocky Mountain Superchair
Independence Superchair

BRECKENRIDGE SKI RESORT

Base Elevation: 9,961'

Vertical Gain to Vista Haus: 1,200'

Breckenridge Ski Resort only allows uphill access outside of operating hours. Nevertheless, access is free, the routes are nice, and the policy is straightforward.

Dogs? Not allowed, except service dogs.

Uphill Pass Required? No. Please wear reflective clothing and be aware of the uphill access parking permit (see below).

Access/Parking: Follow our driving directions for Route 16: Bald Mountain Breckenridge. Free parking is allowed in the North Gondola lot, Stables lot at Peak 8, and the Beaver Run Parking lot between 6 AM and the resort opening time. All cars utilizing these lots will need a free uphill access parking permit. To obtain it, scan the QR code below, or find it at breckpark.com. For evening access, hourly rates and rules apply.

During Operating Hours: Uphill skiing is not allowed during operating hours at Breckenridge.

Non-Operating Hours: You may access the ski area summit outside operating hours from 6 AM to resort opening time. All uphill users must be clear of the mountain by the resort opening time; otherwise, regular parking rates apply. Non-paid users will be ticketed. Ascend and descend only the designated routes. If the route or ski run is not listed below, uphillers may not access it at any time during the ski season. Before uphilling, always check the access hotline by calling 970-547-5627.

- Peak 6: NO UPHILL ACCESS
- Peak 7: Fort Mary B › Claimjumper › Pika › the T-bar hut
- Peak 8: Peak 8 Base › Springmeier › Vista Haus or Claimjumper › Pika › the T-bar hut
- Peak 9: Silverthorne › Lower American › Cashier › Overlook › Peak 9 Patrol Hut
- Peak 10: NO UPHILL ACCESS

Early Season: Early season (and late season), uphill access routes will be limited and are subject to change and/or close on a daily basis. For the safety of guests and employees, all uphill access users must call the Uphill Access Hotline before accessing the mountain.

Dedicated Uphill Route? Yes.

Recommended Route: The most popular and straightforward route is from the Peak 8 Base, straight up Springmeyer (between Chair 5 and Colorado Superchair). Take Springmeyer all the way to Vista Haus. Descend the same route.

Top of Eagle Bahn
Eagle Bahn Gondola
Lions Head

VAIL SKI RESORT

Base Elevation: 8,150’

Vertical Gain to Vista Haus: 2,200’

Vail boasts a dedicated uphill route that begins at Lionshead, a part of the base village. The route is pleasant, but parking can be a hassle, and holiday crowds may be excessive. Nonetheless, Vail has a festive spirit and the uphill route’s summit yields beautiful views of Colorado’s famed Gore mountain range.

Dogs? Not allowed.

Uphill Pass Required? No. Wear reflective clothing.

Vail Uphill Information

Access/Parking: Vail is located just off I-70, 100 miles west of Denver. The resort’s parking situation is too complex to cover here. Refer to internet sources and consider using bus routes to avoid expensive, close-in parking.

During Operating Hours: You cannot uphill ski during operating hours at Vail.

Non-Operating Hours: Follow either of two dedicated routes. Access is permitted from 30 minutes after lift closure until 15 minutes before the first chair. Call the hotline before every tour: 970-754-1023

Dedicated Uphill Route? Yes.

Recommended Route: The most popular and straightforward is from Lionshead up Simba to Eagle’s Nest. There is also a dedicated route from Vail Village up Riva Ridge.

Round-trip: 2.5 mi

SUNLIGHT MOUNTAIN RESORT 28
Lift 2
Lift 3
To Williams Peak p. 36

SUNLIGHT MOUNTAIN RESORT

Base Elevation: 8,230'

Vertical Gain to Summit: 1,640'

Sunlight is known as an affordable and friendly place to ski—both uphill and down. Commodious parking adjacent to the base area is a pleasant perk, as are the area's beautiful aspen forests and lower-altitude warmth. During the formative days of uphill "skimo" ski racing in Colorado, Sunlight had the vision to host an exciting contest that involved competitors proving how many vertical feet they could ski up, and down, in 24 hours. "24 Hours of Sunlight" was held during February of 2006 through 2009, and canceled due to logistical challenges as well as concerns about medical issues with athletes who pushed to the point of organ failure. Who won? In 2008, endurance athlete Eric Sullivan set the then-world record for vertical feet: 51,068. Think about that as you enjoy your pleasant sunny uphill—once, perhaps twice? Sullivan did it 32 times, up and down (in case you do the math, turnaround was somewhat below the summit).

Dogs? Not allowed.

Uphill Pass Required? Yes.
Purchase at ticket window. Wear reflective clothing.

Access/Parking: In Glenwood Springs, drive Grand Avenue/Hwy. 82 and turn onto 27th Street. Continue a short distance over a bridge to a roundabout. At the roundabout, take the second exit, turning right onto South Midland Avenue. Drive Midland Ave. for about a mile to a road fork. Head right at the fork onto Fourmile Road; continue 10 miles to the Sunlight Resort mega-complex. Sunlight access roads are winter-maintained, and snow tires are mandatory. Plentiful parking exists at the base area, as well as a large overflow lot during high season. The popular uphill routes all begin on the snow apron above the base lodge.

Sunlight Uphill Information

All Hours During Winter Season: Sunlight welcomes uphill skiing during all hours, though during holidays they recommend starting an hour before the lifts open or delaying your start until around closing time. Excellent "summit" views reward you, and full-moon tours are popular. A warming room at the summit has remained unlocked for years, so please take care of Sunlight's property so we can retain this amenity.
Before and After Winter Season: Uphilling allowed, all runs.

Dedicated Uphill Route? No.
Recommended Route: Grab a trail map at the resort.The most common route (about 1.3 miles) begins at the obvious base area day-lodge and heads up lower angled terrain to a lift loading station. Trend a bit left here and continue up the Sun King and Little Max trails to the summit lift station. A longer route, excellent for first-timers, follows the 2-mile Ute Trail, accessed by heading westerly from the base area.

To Sugarbowls pg. 36
To Aspen
To Glenwood Springs

BUTTERMILK / TIEHACK MOUNTAIN

Base Elevation: 8,160’

Vertical Gain to Summit: 1,760’

Buttermilk could almost be considered two ski mountains.The “front side,” facing Hwy. 82, is home to an enormous terrain park and excessively low-angled uphilling. Swing around to the east, however, and the Tiehack area provides some of the finest resort uphill skiing in Colorado. It is almost always groomed, with a well-designed designated uphill route. Please patronize the summit restaurant, as this is the resort’s only economic incentive for providing free use of their snow.

Dogs? Only allowed outside operating hours.

Uphill Pass Required? Yes. If you're uphilling Tiehack, purchase passes at the main Buttermilk ticket office, as the Tiehack ticket window is only open intermittently. As of 2021 the pass was $69 and covered the entire season, with no option for a less expensive single-day pass. Uphillers must wear armband.

Access/Parking: Colorado Hwy. 82 is your access. From the city of Glenwood Springs, drive 37 miles to the Buttermilk stoplight. Here, you’re looking at the main, “front” side of Buttermilk—which is not your destination. Continue on Hwy. 82 though the stoplight; after a few hundred yards turn right off Hwy. 82 on Tiehack Road (indicated by a brown and white “Ski Area” sign). Continue for a mile to obvious parking. From Aspen, driving to Tiehack is a bit complex. From the roundabout you hit just west of town, continue for a mile on Hwy. 82 to a right (north) turn onto Stage Road, which leads you away from the skiing. Take another, immediate right turn that leads you through an underpass to the Tiehack Road. The turn off Hwy. 82 is announced with a brown-and-white “Ski Area” sign. If you miss the turn, continue to the stoplight and circle back on Hwy. 82 using the directions above.

During Operating Hours: While dedicated uphill routes are available on the “main” Buttermilk side facing Hwy. 82, as well as on the West Buttermilk side, we recommend the uphilling on the Tiehack side, facing Aspen. The route is well-marked, beginning at the warming hut next to the Tiehack ski lift.

Non-Operating Hours: Use any of the ski runs. Stay away from working machinery and obey closures.

Dedicated Uphill Route? Yes.

Designated Routes: The Tiehack uphill route is well-marked with orange disks, and mandatory during resort operating hours. The frontside and West Buttermilk routes are obvious as well. For a fun tour, ascend Tiehack, ski down West Buttermilk, then climb West Buttermilk and ski down Tiehack to parking. Buttermilk boasts quite a bit of snowmaking. Do not ski over cables or hoses.

Non-Designated Routes: Uphill any run during non-operating hours, with consideration for closures and grooming work.

Buttermilk Uphill Information

Buckeye Platter
10th Mountain Division

SKI COOPER

Base Elevation: 10,530'

Vertical Gain to Summit: 1,220'

Cooper Hill (officially "Ski Cooper") is a smaller resort located near the summit of Tennessee Pass. One of Colorado's oldest ski areas, Cooper has origins in 1942, when the U.S. Army trained the nascent 10th Mountain Division troopers at nearby Camp Hale.The soldiers used Cooper for ski training—it's said they built what was then the longest rope tow in the world. No doubt they also used the area under human power.

Dogs? Not allowed, with the exception of service animals.

Uphill Pass Required? No. You are encouraged to wear reflective clothing and a headlamp.

Access/Parking: Driving to Ski Cooper is easy. Access Hwy. 24 from I-70 on the north (27 miles) or Hwy. 91 on the south (10 miles). Parking may be limited during weekends and on holidays.

During Operating Hours: From 8 AM to 4 PM, opening day through closing day (late November/early December to early April), there are three designated uphill routes, described below.

Non-Operating Hours: Uphilling is allowed on all trails except those that are closed and those on which grooming operations are taking place. See the night's grooming plan and trail report posted on the north side of the lodge next to the exterior First Aid Room door—they try to update it every evening, but cannot guarantee it. The same rules apply after seasonal closure.

Dedicated Uphill Route? Yes.

Designated Route: Looker's left of Trail's End is the front side uphill route; Piney Ditch Road to looker's left of Ambush is the back side uphill route; looker's right of Low Road/High Road to Motherlode Flats is the route from the Tennessee Creek Basin. Follow the yellow and blue Uphill Route signs. If a designated uphill route is closed for any reason, the uphill route may be moved to another trail.

Ski Cooper Uphill Information

To Snow Stake
Top of Barrel Loop
Top of Pano Route
Top of Mirk Route
Breezeway Lift
To Salida

MONARCH MOUNTAIN

Base Elevation: 10,830'

Vertical Gain to Summit: 1,000'

At Monarch, "family-friendly" is an understatement. This resort is a cultural relief from some of the more "glamorous" resorts in the state. While Monarch does not boast a huge amount of vertical, it does have some fantastic exploratory options. Making laps is a breeze; all in-bounds runs bring you right back to one base area. Perfect for childcare swapping.

Dogs? Only allowed outside operating hours.

Uphill Pass Required? Yes.
Monarch season passholders may receive an uphill season ticket at no additional cost, but must sign an uphill travel waiver at the Guest Services desk. All other uphill users must purchase an uphill season ticket for $15 and sign a waiver at the Guest Services desk.

Access/Parking: Monarch is located on Hwy. 50, near the towns of Gunnison and Salida. During off-hours, park near the water treatment facility. Walk to the south end of the base lodge. Mount up here and look for the uphill route/boundary line on your far left, or far right. During periods of heavy use, follow signs.

During Operating Hours: Uphill travel is allowed during operating hours (9 AM to 4 PM), on two designated uphill routes. An uphill pass allows access through the boundary gates. If you are knowledgeable of avalanche safety and equipped with avalanche gear, you may enter and leave the resort boundary at one of three access points.

1. East of the summit of Old Monarch Pass along the Roundabout Trail, just below the Curecanti Trail.
2. Near the top of the Panorama lift, at the top of the Great Divide Trail.
3. In the Mirkwood Basin, at the bottom of Elation Ridge along the boundary line.

Non-Operating hours: Outside of operating hours, Monarch uphill travel is allowed on all trails within the ski area boundary with the following exceptions:

- Terrain parks (closed at all times)
- Mirkwood and other avalanche terrain (may be closed—respect signs and/or ropes)
- Terrain where avalanche mitigation, special events, administrative closures, or construction and maintenance activities are taking place (closed as necessary)

Dedicated Uphill Route? Yes—three options.
Recommended Route: Basically, ski clockwise along the ski area boundary. Start on the dedicated uphill at the lower lift (Garfield) up the center of Lower Tango, to climber's right of North Forty, to the top of Gunbarrel. The ski area calls this "The Barrell Loop." Descend from there. Or to continue your circumnavigation of the resort, travel north along the Continental Divide with or without skins, depending on your style. Throw your skis on your pack and bootpack up to Mirkwood Basin (if the gate is open), drop Elation Ridge and skate the cat-track back to the base area. Mirkwood is all ungroomed double black diamond. It is not friendly to tiny race skis, but it's a good zone for advanced-skill adventure.

Monarch Mountain Uphill Information

Round-trip: 3 mi

Whetstone Mountain
Paradise Express
Daytime Route
Red Lady Express

CRESTED BUTTE MOUNTAIN RESORT

Base Elevation: 9,370’

Vertical Gain to Summit: 1,750’

Crested Butte Mountain Resort has a robust uphill skiing program. You can travel (with a pass) on the dedicated routes at any time, unless they’re closed for avalanche control or maintenance. During daytime hours, plan to spend time at the umbrella bar along the route for wide views, food and drink.

Dogs?
Only allowed outside operating hours. Dogs must wear a collar light.

Uphill Pass Required? Yes. Acquire at the base-area ticket office.

Access/Parking: If you're a newcomer to this area, note that the resort bears the same name as the town of Crested Butte, which is located in the valley southwest of the ski hill. The best access to the ski slopes is by bus from town to the resort's base area. From there, walk to the bottom of the Red Lady chairlift and begin your uphill. Alternatively, you can usually find free parking outside of operating hours by driving towards the resort from town. Before you reach the ski area, turn right on Hunter Hill Road. Stay left until you see the dirt lot on your left. Access the base area from this lot by crossing the street and walking up the covered stairway.

During Operating Hours: Uphill travel is NOT allowed during operating hours (9 AM to 4 PM). CBMR and Vail Resorts discontinued daytime uphilling in 2020.

Before and after operating hours: The area is open outside of operating hours, but only via a designated route. You are required to wear a headlamp at all times. When the Ski Patrol is conducting early morning avalanche control work, a red light will be deployed on tower 3 of the Red Lady lift and at the base area.

DO NOT CONTINUE UPHILL BEYOND YELLOW BRICK ROAD AT UPPER PARK!

Dedicated Uphill Route? Yes.

After the resort closes for the season:

Designated Route Outside of Operating Hours: Warming House Hill › Lower Keystone › Upper Park › Yellow Brick Road › Paradise Bowl › Silver Queen Road › Windy Gap. The descent route is restricted to the same trails, in reverse. Until the upper mountain is open down to Upper Park, do not proceed uphill past the junction of Peanut and Lower Keystone. During early season ramp up, a sign will indicate this specific area.

Designated Route During Operating Hours: Warming House Hill to Lower Keystone to Houston Canyon; at intersection of Houston Canyon and Splain’s Gulch the route heads into the trees of Columbine Hill and meanders through trees to top of Homeowners trail at top of Painter Boy/Gold Link lifts and Umbrella Bar at Ten Peaks. From Umbrella Bar at Ten Peaks you can continue on to the edge of the trees at Bubba’s Ski Way. At this point, there may be signs telling you not to continue farther. Signs or not, this is basically the top of the route, and a good place to rip your skins and head down the groomers.

Special note from Ski Patrol:

Winch Cat grooming operations – Dangerous cable! Under no circumstances may anyone access any area within the Resort where winch cat operations are taking place. Such work involves cables stretched tightly across the terrain and is very dangerous. Skiing into or near the cables can result in serious injury or death. Respect strobe lights and signage.

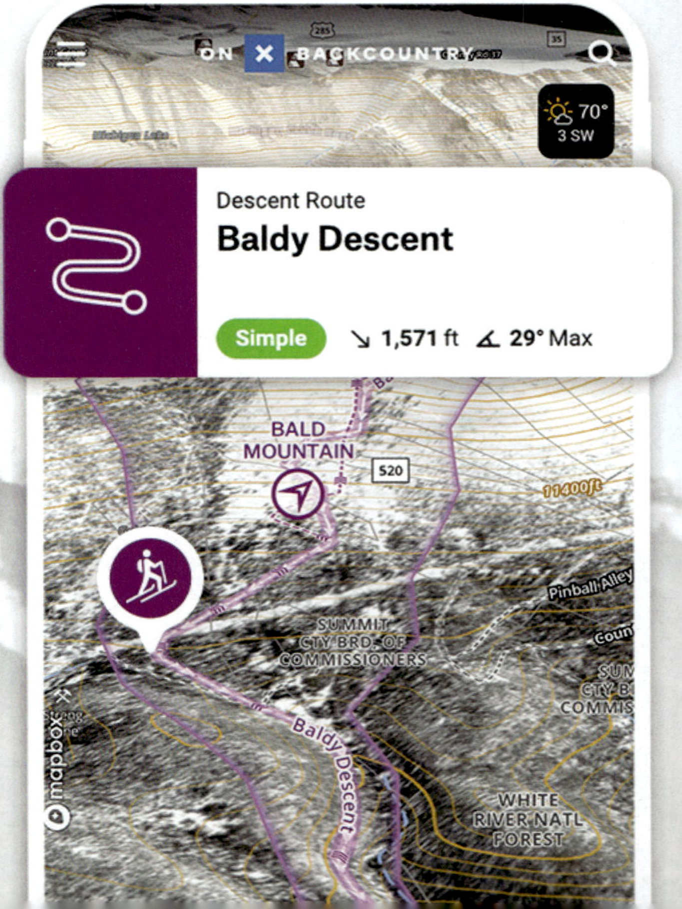
ON BACKCOUNTRY
70°
3 SW
Descent Route
Baldy Descent
Simple
1,571 ft
29° Max
BALD MOUNTAIN
520
11400ft
Pinball Alley
SUMMIT CTY BRD. OF COMMISSIONERS
Baldy Descent
WHITE RIVER NATL FOREST
mapbox

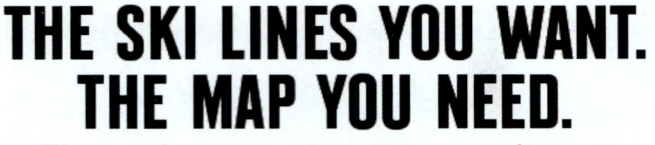